Cou to dream...

...the impossible becomes reality

Coralita Martin with Sandie Shirley

Lastword Publications
Lowestoft, Suffolk, UK
www.lastwordpublications.com

First published 2010, by Lastword Publications
www.lastwordpublications.com
Lastword Publications works with authors and musicians, businesses and charities to provide professional results with maximum impact.

ISBN: 978-0-9559439-4-2

Design and production by The Upper Room (London, UK) +44 (0)20 8406 1010

Dedication

I dedicate this book to my heavenly Father, the author and finisher of my life, in praise and love for all the wonderful things he has done. To my youngest son, a companion and friend; to my daughter, a help and inspiration to be a teacher in the UK; and to the rest of my children – I love them all through the heartaches, joys and sorrows, and I know they love me. To my friend Denise, who has been like a mother and sister to me.

Some names and places have been changed to protect identities.

Coralita *August 2010*

Foreword

Coralita Martin was wearing a woollen hat pulled down over her ears. She was barely five feet tall but she was big on personality, with an infectious laugh. At more than 70 years old, she was doing what she liked most – teaching children. She was putting a collage together with large and small at the local church youth group in a deprived overspill town: Thetford, Norfolk, England.

As a reporter, I thought it was a routine, low-key story for the weekly paper, but I had stumbled on a woman with an epic biography of enduring faith mined in the deep caverns of suffering that bore God's signature. Terrible tragedy has forged an invincible, winning spirit in Coralita that will bring hope to every bankrupt, hurting soul.

She was born in Antigua in the West Indies. Poor, rejected, misused and abused, she did not even own a pair of shoes. Against the odds she won a school scholarship: the first stage of her dream to become a teacher. With grit and determination she has turned the countless trials of homelessness, rape, an abusive, violent marriage and near-death into golden miles. Forced to trade the sunny shores of Antigua, where she knew now-famous singer and songwriter Joan Armatrading, for the grime of East End London, she faced racism and endless hardship.

But Coralita is a victor and not a victim. Faith, courage, strength, forgiveness and an angel encounter from an almighty God has broken the mould of prejudice, poverty and injustice that gripped this woman's life.

For 50 years she has opened the annals of learning for thousands of youngsters who still hold her dear. Teaching has spanned the generations and cultures, taking her on the fast track to success from a private school in the Caribbean to tough inner London schools, salubrious fee-paying ones and a variety in Norfolk. Often the children's first black teacher, she has taught future doctors, lawyers, entrepreneurs and even convicted criminals. She has dined with rich, influential parents and cried tears for the youngsters downtrodden by abuse, fear and poverty as they have struck a strong chord of empathy.

Coralita is a beacon of hope for her native Caribbean people and those the world over as she has found favour with God and mankind in the fierce battles for survival that tore at her life from birth.

This is a story of loss and gain, pain and hardship. A story of victory over poverty; love over hate; and peace over fear. It is a story that will challenge and change your life for ever.

Jesus looked at them and said: "With man this is impossible, but with God all things are possible." Matthew 19: 26 (NIV)

(When God is all you have, God is all you need!)

Sandie Shirley

Courage to dream

Contents

1 Poor and disowned — 3

2 Learning is sweet — 13

3 Pathway to the future — 29

4 Eviction and peril — 37

5 Passage to England — 49

6 Hostels, hovels and havens — 57

7 A teacher's footsteps — 71

8 A new learning curve — 81

9 Angel encounter — 93

10 Prime position — 111

11 Island of change — 123

12 Favour or furore — 129

13 Deliverance — 135

14 Never retiring — 141

References — 148

Chapter 1 **Poor and disowned**

Life shrinks or expands according to one's courage.
Anais Nin [1]

There was always mounting excitement, splashing through the shallows towards the deep. I did not think about the sharks. I was eager to reach the food boat laden with mangoes and bananas. Risking life itself, I swam to greet it, ready to gorge on fruit that sometimes made me sick during the long swim back. Even at nine years old, I had spirit.

I was a child beyond my years. An adventurer, an inventor, a budding entrepreneur when I was just knee-high; bright in the classroom and adept in the market place – business acumen honed with skill and cunning. I was all these things in order to silence the gnawing hunger in my stomach.

I was born in Antigua – a Caribbean Island that rises like a verdant jewel in the turquoise waters. It boasts 365 beaches – one for every day of the year! But beneath the beauty was a glaring dark divide. The trade winds that blew across its shores brought colonial affluence but also underscored poverty and hardship: poverty that could callous and steal the soul; poverty that could demean humanity. It would bring a quiet and certain indignation, a determination to wrench off its stranglehold. A resolve to fight the injustice and prejudice that was mine from birth.

My mother was eighteen when I was born out of wedlock. At ten days old, with an eye infection, I was discarded like an unwanted animal. Thrown out onto the dewy grass, I was just another statistic to vex the tight family budget. I was named after the crimson flower that appears in June. I came into the world in 1933 – a world that began without grace or privilege. A world that owed me nothing.

I was rescued by my godmother, Agatha. She lived in a tiny two-bedroom house by the beach, near St John's – the capital, on the north side of the island. Like the other slum houses, it had a corrugated tin roof that magnified the sound of the pounding winter rains. Roses, frangipane and irises clung to the dusty tracks, their scented beauty a marked contrast to the squalor of the lowly one-storeys with their flaking paint and weathered timber. There was no kitchen, bathroom or electricity. We cooked and washed outside, using a standpipe to rinse away the daily grime and sweat.

I shared Agatha's home with her children and slept on a sheet on the floor in the living area. Sometimes a foul stench would hang in the hot dry air where the homesteads were wedged close together.

There was a yard for the washing line and an open fire for cooking, when the salt air became pungent with fish. Crab, red mullet, shark, grouper and snapper – the staple diet was eaten with rice or dumplings, or made into a hearty soup. Meat was bought on special occasions when a pig or lamb was killed in the village. We ate okra, aubergines, yams, sweet potatoes, sugar apple, cassata and the sweetest pineapples – they grew beneath the wide sapphire skies, streaked by the setting sun.

It was a world set apart from the wealth of the colonial trade barons. Their grandiose living came from the sugar and rum exported to England for centuries, but it meant stark, cruel living for native West Indians. Hunched backs, worn fingers and sweating faces testified to the weariness that came and stayed as my people laboured for their masters' rich profits in sizzling temperatures.

Reform began to sweep over the West Indies in the 1930s, causing political unrest. Cornwall Bird – a black public school pupil and Salvation Army Captain – would be groomed to help resurrect the lives of poor, working-class black Caribbeans.

Destined to shift the political, economic and social power, he would help lead the country out of the feudal colonial system into democracy. But it would be a long, enduring pathway of change spanning decades before Antigua's independence in 1968. He would spearhead the transition with minimal violence – unlike other parts of the West Indies, where there was bloodshed, riots and a state of emergency.

He would influence the times as a pioneer of the Antigua Trades and Labour Union. After years of bitter negotiation and imprisonment of some of its members, he would be the chief bargainer against the old established order, helping to forge Caribbean Free Trade. Known fondly as Papa Bird – kind and compassionate, a tireless fighter for the rights of the masses – he would become the architect of the island's industrial peace and progress, laying the groundwork for its prosperity. He would later become Antigua's first premier and be known as the Honourable Vere Cornwall Bird. His life's mission of liberation and change for every underprivileged Caribbean would progress slowly. For me it would come too late.

Under the influential wing of Aunt Agatha, I was sheltered from the ravages of poverty during my early years. Agatha, with her compassionate wide eyes and fair skin, was god-fearing and wise. She underpinned right living, strict discipline and a simple faith in Jesus. At night, for as long as I can remember, I knelt before my makeshift bed to say the same simple prayer:

Heavenly Father, hear my cry.
Lord protect me through the night and keep me safe till morning light.
God bless my mother, father, grandfather. God bless everybody.

On Sunday mornings, in my best dress, I went to church and recited from the Anglican prayer book. During the afternoons, English or American missionaries held a Sunday school in the nearby playground. I learnt quickly, poring over my memory verse with a neighbour, Aunt Helena, every week. Thirty-five years later, during a return visit from England, that same old aunt sat on the veranda outside her little shack. The palm trees swayed in the gentle breeze circling the white sands as I passed by.

"Coralita, Coralita," cried Aunt Helena, her dusky face creased and smiling when she saw me. "Come and say your memory verse."

Old habits died hard in Antigua – habits that were often passed down through the generations to turn the financial wheels of self-sufficiency. From a young age I dredged the nearby shallow coastal waters for cockles. Cooked and eaten, the pearly pink, yellow and green shells were then drilled with holes and strung together to make bracelets and necklaces. I stood on the jetty, watching and waiting for the ships packed with tourists to arrive as regularly as the weekly tides. I held out the souvenirs in ready anticipation as the finely dressed men and women made their way down the gangplank. Before long the trinkets were changing hands for a dollar or fifty cents – enough for a full square meal.

My fingers were deft and nimble, threading the tiny shells in quick succession. But once I swallowed the needle when I put it between my teeth with gritted determination to string the shells. There was a commotion as Agatha carried me on a speedy visit to the doctor that resulted in a prescribed meal of cotton wool and porridge to ensure it was passed without injury.

At four I was competent at many household tasks. I would sweep, clean and wash. I only had two dresses; so washing was a frequent task, in a huge bath made from hardened mud (later replaced by a tin one), filled with water from the standpipe. With two pence worth of soap bought from the local shop, I would wash and rinse repeatedly, then finally "blue" the wash with a tiny muslin bag of dye to keep my garments fresh and white. It was a painstaking ritual, before the wet clothes were wrung out and put on the line or fence to dry.

I learnt to respect my elders, not questioning or answering back. I was schooled in life's lessons that were seldom forgotten when taught with gentle persuasion by Agatha.

"You must not tell lies. What can you learn from a liar? What can you learn from a thief? You don't have to steal anything, you just have to ask," she said.

I loved Agatha. I saw a depth to her soul that was harnessed by faith. There was no-one to match her tenderness and love. She instilled a solid foundation in God. Whether it was knocked this way or that, it could not be rocked; rather it would grow like a strong oak tree during the harsh years of suffering that followed.

Those happy, carefree days were snatched away when I was six. My mother Ketura, who had to be known as Ketty, and never mother, wanted me back. My cries and sobs made no difference to her decision. To this day I never really understood why she wanted me. Was there a quarrel between the two families, who lived only doors apart? Or was it to fetch water and wood and scrub the floor?

The separation gouged a deep, seeping wound across my heart. I did not know where I belonged. Trust and security were gone, but my anguish was met with angry words.

"If you ever go near your godmother again, I will tie you with a rope so you never get to see her," said Ketty.

Agatha and I would sometimes pass each other on the street where we lived. With tear-filled eyes we were forced to act as if we were strangers.

There was little to shield me from the harsh effects of being poor when I moved in with Ketty and my sisters, Evelyn and Jackie. Prejudice thrived under the family roof. While I ate the crumbs, my siblings enjoyed the best. They called me Secondhand Rose in the family hand-me-downs. I never owned a pair of shoes until I was a teenager, and there were no regular meals. The prime meat and fish portions were never mine. When my father, who died when I was six, killed a pig, I was given the trotters to eat. When fish was served I was given the head, with the brain. That included the prized jackfish that I found swimming in the freshwater mangroves or were caught by night-time fishermen, who blew their conch shells in triumph when one was landed.

Ketty's fish soup was renowned. Its enticing smell drew people from across the neighbourhood to sample the hot broth. Despite the poverty, there was plenty for others in a traditional culture that shared and gave – a culture that perplexed and saddened me, since I was often hungry.

When there was no food on the table, Ketty turned on me.

"Why did you not go to Miss Pansy and get some credit?" she cried.

I knew better than to go to the grocer's without permission; so Ketty had to go instead, which made her angry.

"When I get this food and cook it, don't think you are going to get any," shouted Ketty.

I learnt not to question the status quo or presume any better. It was a house governed by the strictest rules. They had to be observed.

My stomach often ached for food. I never seemed to make the grade with Ketty, who held the keys to the larder and the financial purse strings for everything else. I did not know what provoked the obvious dislike, but I firmly believed my mother never really loved me.

There were many things I did not understand, including the family outing to the cinema. Evelyn, who was three years older, was taken on the back of my father's motorbike, while I had to walk. My sister sat in the posh seats in the circle with our father, while I sat alone in the stalls, crouching in fear at the odd black-and-white Charlie Chaplin movie. More than 60 years later I am still afraid to go to the cinema alone.

To keep starvation away I needed to be inventive. After school I sneaked off to the nearby sugar factory with an old bean tin I customised with a pourer. Once inside the building, and under cover of the dimly lit interior, I hurried to the rows of sugar bags. I drilled a tiny hole in one of the bags with my finger and let the contents trickle into the can. I would run from the factory to the nearby standpipe to make a satisfying sweet drink with water before bedtime. Sometimes the sugar was dirty, and the drink was a sludge-grey colour, so I strained it through the end of my cotton dress, which I washed afterwards. When I did not visit the factory I went to sleep on the floor with an empty stomach – and woke in the morning full of wind!

For money I scoured the neighbourhood for glass bottles, which I washed and sold for a dollar each (equivalent to an English penny). I bought a carton of mauby – a nutritious drink for breakfast – and a coconut tart for lunch. When there were no bottles to wash, there was no morning or midday meal.

I would run errands clad in my simple, fading summer dress. My bare feet pounded the dirt road. I was fit and athletic – breaking into a run across the beach as I splashed along the water's edge or sped between the vegetation that was lush and green from the torrential winter rains – rains that sometimes seeped through my little windswept home, which stood perilously close to extinction during the hurricane season. Rains that would soak my night-time sheet airing outside in the balmy temperatures, so that I was forced to spend the dark night huddled in a corner of the house.

There was little respite for my work-weary hands, which collected wood for the open fire and heaved the awkward water container from the standpipe night and day. They were sore and chafed from the endless demands of emptying Ketty's commode in the sea and scrubbing the wooden floor that took the assault from the family's shoes.

At times I was bruised and bitter from the injustice. One day, I believed, I would escape and be a lady. I would eat with a knife and fork, instead of my fingers and spoon, by an open fire that left my clothes smelling of smoke. I borrowed a book about etiquette when I could read. I clutched it like a prized possession during my regular visits to the beach. Away from prying eyes I opened the pages and read intently as I laid an imaginary place for dinner.

"Knives to the right, forks to the left. Tip the soup bowl away from you."

I held a pretend dainty tea cup and crooked my little finger. I had dreams for a better life that would transport me into genteel living, silver service, a wider vocabulary and a job above all jobs. I vowed I would never be a servant, a shop girl or a plantation worker. I dreamed big dreams as I watched the sunsets light the horizon and walked across the soft white sand that flowed between my toes.

They were dreams that put a fire in my heart as I chose to be a victor and not a victim. With gutsy determination I made the most and best of everything. Maybe it was this attitude that bred resentment within the family. Despite being obedient, hardworking and keen to mind my own business, there were frequent outbursts from Ketty.

"Don't look at me with those eyes. You have got wicked eyes," she ranted.

If I erred, there was a beating with a stick.

"Come over here. Why did you do such a terrible thing?" Ketty would bawl.

With every word there was a stroke. When I cried there was another outburst of anger.

"Stop your crying!"

I met my only friend Molly at Sunday school. She lived a long walk away across the wide breach that divided the slums from the fine homes with their nearby park and clean wide roads. Molly's parents had money. They owned a grocery shop stacked with more items than I could have imagined. It adjoined their house, with its splendid dimensions and hanging garden. There was polished furniture, a fitted kitchen, bathroom and a dining table set with the best crockery, silver cutlery and bulging fruit bowl. I would make regular Sunday visits for tea, where I practised my etiquette with ease.

Lazy afternoons were spent in the cool shade of Molly's yard beneath the canopied trees and riots of coloured roses and irises. Molly would entertain me, letting me choose from the huge sweet jars in the shop. I suspected that she also dropped the sixpences in the yard which she encouraged me to find and take home. But I never invited Molly for a return visit where the air was bad and the living unlovely. I was too ashamed.

We shared our dreams and secrets and recounted our heartaches. We went to the little Moravian church – the Church of the Caribbean – sang hymns and learnt scripture. We joined confirmation classes, and when we both became church members we recited the same verse that we chose together.

Our friendship was like soldering silver amid the alternating chapters on the way from childhood to adulthood, making us a crutch for one another. Molly would later become a head teacher, with a husband. They would live in a fine American-style house with a wide veranda that later became the private school that she ran.

Chapter 2 Learning is sweet

The stronger the winds, the deeper the roots and the longer the winds, the more beautiful the tree. Charles Swindoll [2]

My step was light and carefree as I set out for school for the first time on a memorable late summer's day. There was no hint of nerves or apprehension. With my head held high, I strode confidently beside my sister Evelyn towards the far from salubrious Point Government School that served the poor surrounding neighbourhood.

The two-storey wooden building was close to the railway line that took the train, loaded with sugar cane, from the fields to the grocery stores and rum factory. Soon I would witness a terrible, unforgettable scene when dozens of children dared, as they always did, to climb aboard the passing goods train to grasp the sugar cane sticks. On that day the sun would darken. The cheers and smiles would cease. One small child would lose his footing and fall under the wheels of the moving train. There would be a reverent hush on that day, and many afterwards, in memory of the boy who lost his legs for the sake of a sweet piece of cane.

But today I was oblivious to such terror. I was about to embrace learning like a mother embraces her new-born child. I had a winning attitude that had been fused through necessity and now it would see me outshine my contemporaries. There was a resilience, together with a teachable spirit, to see me reach for God's glory not only in the classroom but across the athletics arena.

Knowledge would become a priority both inside and outside of the classroom. I would draw it towards me in huge mouthfuls, ravenous for more, visiting the library after school to gulp down the words of some of Britain's great poets.

The gate to knowledge that beckoned would make me upwardly mobile for the rest of my life. My school days became some of my happiest. An industrious worker, clever thinker and careful planner, I would be rewarded with rapid class promotion years ahead of my time. But coupled with my obvious poverty, I would feel the full brunt of resentment from competing pupils. It would mean isolation and rejection. Yet despite everything I did not have, I would know and understand with increasing assurance that I was blessed with brains that were no longer concentrating solely on surviving the scandalous poverty.

Yet it was poverty I had to contend with even before the school day began. It marked a pre-school ritual of waking early while Jackie and Evelyn continued sleeping. The sunlight would bathe my face as it shone through the glass louvre shutters of the little one-bedroom shack. I heard the whispered hush of the ocean as I opened my eyes. I would listen intently and smile, strangely comforted by its familiarity. Stretching my legs and yawning, I rose from the makeshift bed on the wooden floor, scooped up my cotton sheet and hung it on the line to air outside.

Next door the sound of an unbolted stall broke the peace. I waited expectantly. In another moment the usual clatter of goats' hooves filled the air. Gradually the noise lessened and faded as they careered down the road to graze at St John's Cathedral on Newgate Street and Long Street, before returning at sunset.

I washed at the outside standpipe – the water was ice cold, banishing the last traces of tiredness before I returned to the house. Without a murmur to anyone in the quietened early morning, I put on the faded hand-me-down frock I had washed the night before. Leaving the cool interior I met the dazzling sunlight outside again, surveying nature's panorama beyond the peculiar, rickety community. I would often stand on that veranda for a few moments, delighted by the sheer beauty of the ocean, serene and sparkling below the waking summer sky.

Reluctantly, I would leave for the dust track into the country and a mammoth four-hour sales mission to help with Ketty's fruit and vegetable business. It took an hour to collect the fresh produce and carry it back on a tray on my head. Rather than use the three pennies she gave me for the bus fare, I bought butter, cheese and freshly baked bread for breakfast during the journey.

Ketty knew I was an asset. Young, fit and quick on my feet, I also had a gilt-edged sales tongue; so on my return, she used me to visit neighbouring customers. I had a likeable demeanour and knew what to say; so sales were swift. But my efforts did not bring a kind response from Ketty – there was still no praise, breakfast or payment for my work.

Instead my ability meant more graft before school. I would sell another tray of produce for Ketty's friend, Mama Mady, learning this time to turn the job to my advantage. Mama Mady would say: "I want you to sell four bananas for a dollar." Instead I sold three bananas for a dollar and collected a fruit surplus to sell, keeping the profit. But I was always careful that Mama Mady received what she expected.

On a typical school day I had risen before dawn to be my mother's business dealer. There were still beads of sweat in the creases of my brown eyes when I reached the noisy classroom by nine o'clock. Relieved, I eased myself between the familiar pupils on the long bench seat, shifting into an upright, alert position, to take up my slate and begin lessons.

By the time I was ten, I was in the third standard, having moved from the crowded open-plan classroom on the lower floor and climbed the wooden steps to the upper storey. Reading, writing and arithmetic were mastered with competence and understanding, yet I could still be distracted.

There was a gentle breeze blowing through the class from an open window as Mr Porter explained long division on the blackboard. But I was not listening. I played intently with my dice, rolling it back and forth across the desk, studying the numbers thrown. Mr Porter evidently saw me from the corner of his eye. He turned round sharply. Slowly and deliberately, he walked towards me, standing in front of my desk and holding my gaze with an angry stare.

"Give the dice to me," he barked.

"No, it is mine," I answered.

"Give it to me," he continued fiercely.

"No, it is mine."

Mr Porter dragged the dice out of my hand and slapped me across the face.

I sat in silent indignation. With the gloating, mocking eyes of other children turned towards me, I wanted to escape. Instead I began to plan my reprisal. Ketty would give anyone a fight for their money if she was roused, I reasoned. With this constant thought, I waited until the lesson finished and bounded out of the classroom, down the stairs, two at a time, and across the school grounds towards home.

Ketty was busy in the yard with the washing when I arrived. Bracing myself, I walked towards her, rehearsing my words. "Ketty, I was not doing anything, and dear Mr Porter, he slapped me across the face."

The words relayed the distorted tale. Ketty was immediately rankled. Her lips tightened, and a frown dug across her brow. Without further comment she gathered herself together. With a firm hand on my shoulder she marched me back to school, through the wooden entrance and up the stairs before bustling me into the classroom and beside Mr Porter's desk as he was teaching. He was neither bemused nor fazed. Instead, he looked up from his class and turned towards Ketty, who looked at him forcibly in the eye.

"Mr Porter, what did Coralita do?"

"I was teaching long division and she was not paying attention; so I just gave her a little tap," he answered.

No more words were exchanged. Ketty took the punishment belt from Mr Porter. She ran her hand down its long, lean length as I inwardly shuddered. Without further hesitation she lashed me without remorse in front of the class of seventy pupils. Then she gave the belt back to Mr Porter and left in silence.

With a pain that throbbed across my limbs, I turned to Mr Porter, punished and humiliated.

"Mr Porter, you can kick me, you can thump me, you can beat me. You can do whatever you like with me, but I am never going to tell my Mum again."

Similar punishment produced another stain of shame across my mind when I was hauled in front of the whole school. I never had a swimming costume like many of the other children, although bathing was a popular lunchtime or after-school pastime. Being poor, I made my knickers from a flour bag bleached in the sun and threaded with string around the waist. I regularly stripped down to my knickers to swim. I was a tomboy, more comfortable with the boys in my class than the girls. Together we swam, climbed trees, played marbles and used a stone and a shaved-down piece of wood to play cricket until it got too dark. Despite being at the top of the school, I was slight and under-developed. I saw no harm in wearing just my knickers to swim regularly with the boys I started First Grade with.

I was seven when I learnt to swim in the waters that had once claimed the life of a young schoolboy during an afternoon swim. I did so by resting across my younger companion's arms, then began to float, instinctively extending my arms and using my legs like flippers to find new freedom. It had been a regular recreation ever since, but now it would be used to ridicule me. In front of 600 pupils, Mr Hall, the headmaster, stood on the school platform with his protruding pot-belly.

"I would like to see Coralita because I was told that she was swimming naked with the boys," he barked.

A tight knot grew in my stomach as I wrestled with the lie. Head bowed with embarrassment, I shuffled between the rows of pupils to the end of the line. Without looking up, I approached the imposing figure that towered above me on the platform. He was highly respected by staff and pupils and known to be fair but also firm, training a child with the rod. In front of the stares of every pupil on the school roll, he took off his belt and used it purposefully – each stroke aimed to deter every silent, watchful child from similar behaviour. It also struck a poignant note of caution for those who held a place of privilege in the school, since I was also a prefect.

The wounding stick of discipline against raw flesh was felt by many. It came easily and sometimes for little reason. Evelyn and I once shared the same class when we studied comparative adjectives for English lessons. Mr Hammond turned towards Evelyn as he stood beside her and shot an unsuspecting question like a poison arrow.

"What are the comparisons for good?" he asked.

"Good, gooder and goodest," she replied.

Without warning he removed his belt, carefully adjusted his shirt cuffs, and lashed her nineteen times – a lash for every word of his response.

"Good, better, better, best – never let it rest until your good is better and your better is your best."

Evelyn was sore and vexed for days afterwards.

There was more to follow when I sat next to Phyllis during the compound fraction lessons. She had a habit of copying everything I wrote – until she had a rude awakening. On one occasion I decided to allow Phyllis to copy the wrong answers and then quickly amended them before the work was inspected by the teacher.

"Well done, Coralita," said Mr Hammond as he assessed my work.

Then he reached for Phyllis' book. His eyes scanned the page rapidly. He gave the book back with a look of contempt.

"You have got every sum wrong."

Phyllis was adamant. "No, I haven't. I have got the same as Coralita," she argued.

"No you haven't. I rubbed them all out," I said, turning towards her with a mischievous grin.

Phyllis was publicly lashed that day. She never cheated again.

The strict regimes were seasoned with patience and kindness. Miss Christopher took a liking to me. She saw hope and potential, despite my poor, lacklustre appearance. At the end of one particular month she approached me with a perceptive smile and pressed some coins into my hand.

"I am going to give you two shillings and sixpence to buy some wool, and I am going to teach you how to knit baby bootees," she insisted.

Without arguing, I bought the wool and with Miss Christopher's expert tuition learnt to ply the needles. I was good at needlework and crafts, so soon mastered the additional skill. Until then I had made 'flycatchers' from coloured tissue paper for Christmas decorations. I would take orders in advance and use customers' deposits to keep a ready supply of paper and cardboard to cut and thread on the beach after school, working quickly to claim sales.

Encouraged by Miss Christopher, I knitted four pairs of bootees for her to sell at her sister's shop, and earned ten shillings. The money bought mangoes and ice-cream and provided savings. Knitting opened up a flourishing livelihood. I would repair fishing nets and knit new ones, finding brisk business on an island that relied on its fishing industry.

Miss Christopher continued to open doors of opportunity. I was in the top class at junior school when the teachers left their classrooms to take exams. Every year they chose some eleven-year-olds to teach the younger ones, and I was selected. I had always wanted to be a teacher but never dared to hope against the odds.

I stood in front of 40 children – some with shoes and socks, others barefoot like me. I came to life with a quick tongue to deliver the lessons I had learnt in the classroom. I could engage with every child, using wit and enthusiasm to hold their attention.

It was a position that sat squarely on my small but formidable shoulders. For the first time I began to hold on to my dream to be a teacher. It was not impossible, I reasoned, to open the annals of learning for others that came after me. A knowing came to the fore of my spirit. I began to speak it out of my mouth with faith and conviction when Uncle Albert, a regular school visitor, saw me.

"Hello little barefoot teacher," he called.

With growing dignity, I rose to my full stature.

"One of these days I am going to show you that I am going to be a proper teacher," I announced.

There was a cruel and bitter blow to come. A few months later I sat the scholarship examinations for secondary school. I was successful. I was one of five girls on the island to gain a celebrated place at the Antigua Girls' High School to further my education. I was notified by letter and summoned with Ketty to an interview. History was rewritten. I was the first child from the slums to earn such a place.

We left the stark ghetto surroundings to the cheers of well-wishers as we headed towards the changing landscape. The run-down buildings and yards littered with goats, cows and chickens gave way to tree-lined boulevards with plush, glass-fronted shops. White colonial buildings were set back from the road with red and purple bougainvillea as we passed the unfamiliar suburbs to the foremost girls' school on the island. A school that had carved the grey matter of thousands of aspiring and elite pupils for decades.

We sat opposite the sombre-faced interviewer, who was shuffling papers when we arrived. On the surface the interview was pleasant. The questions were searching but not difficult to answer. But a week later there was another letter. It was abrupt and uncompromising.

My heart lurched as Ketty read it:

Dear Miss Stewart

I am sorry to say that although you have a place at the Antigua Girls' High School, it will not be possible for you to join the school. Due to your family's financial circumstances, you do not have the means to provide the necessary uniform and books to undertake learning at this establishment. I am afraid to say, we have no alternative but to offer the place to someone else.

My path was barred. My dream of teaching was halted. There was a lump in my throat. I looked down at my thin summer dress and my bare feet, feeling loathing and disappointment. The wide chasm between the poor and the rich had stolen my future.

Ketty put the letter down. Turning to me with a long, disdainful look, she hurled her venom: "If you were a boy I would have sold one of my houses and paid for you to go to high school. But girls, all they bring is bastards; so I am not going to waste my money on you."

Ketty had little to her name, but she did own two shacks in the community. They were no bigger than a small room, but they could have secured my future.

Despite the pain, I did not let it thwart my progress. I continued to grasp every succeeding opportunity, and success came relatively easily. I won elocution competitions, poetry recitations, drama awards and took the starring role as Portia in Shakespeare's Merchant of Venice, which was the school play. I was also famous for my sporting ability.

Fifty schools would gather for Antigua's inter-schools athletics cup at St John's Pavilion every summer. As the event approached, Mr Hammond insisted that I entered every one of the nine races, since the school had never won the event. I readily agreed. There was a secret desire to please the man who awakened my love of words with fabled poets such as Keats, Tennyson and Wordsworth.

On a momentous day, when the sun drenched the grasslands and the overhanging boughs brought welcome shade, I braced myself for the demanding schedule – relay, 80 and 100 metres, sack race, three-legged race, needle-and-cotton race and more besides. I was fit and strong and also disciplined, I knew the importance of stamina and strategy through my own race for survival. It stood me in good stead that day.

With my heart beating wildly, I had my eyes on the finishing line at the start of each event – sprinting, jumping and threading my way to victory every time. I was praised and honoured by every watching adult and child. It was the happiest day of my life. I was lifted high on the shoulders of the other children and carried from the pavilion to my school on the far side of the island. The parading cheers behind me were accompanied by a huge tray heaped with winnings – cookware, glassware and porcelain, a prize for every race I won.

"We want Coralita. We want Coralita. Coralita won the cup," they shouted.

There was barely time to reflect on the day before the winnings were gone. Cradling them in my arms as though they were new toys, I arrived home to find Mrs Brown visiting. She was Ketty's godmother, who lived in a big house on the other side of the community. She eyed the glassware with an envious stare. Taking the dishes, she stroked her clumsy fingers across their circumference.

"Mmmm. I like these."

"Then you can have them," said Ketty, without consulting me.

I was speechless. But further injustice came later that afternoon, when I was sent out to sell the remaining prizes to enlarge the family budget. With a heavy heart I approached the doorways of stranger, foe and neighbour, waxing dutifully and lyrically, meeting the gaze of every potential customer. Some offered only half their value; so I pressed on, halting at each door until, in the cool of the evening, I received a full return for every prize.

A dark shadow of despair passed over me that night. I was inconsolable. There was no escape from injustice. I mused on the misery it brought, including school lunchtimes, when I walked across the nearby beach alone and hungry, unable to afford a meal like other children. Too ashamed to admit the truth, I returned to lessons, pretending I had eaten, wiping my mouth in a mock gesture. I had an astute mind from God. Thanks to Aunt Agatha, I had trusted him as my provider, instructor, mentor and intervener, sustaining me in the darkest hours. I needed his help now.

But the pain was short-lived. My sports prowess was about to
be further commended when I received an invitation to the
annual athletics meeting at Government House, where the
Island's Governor, Lord Baldwin, lived.

I felt tiny and insignificant entering the gates and seeing the
imposing mansion. It lay like a sleeping, imperial giant until a
steady troupe of VIPs were ushered through its doors with the
advancing seasons. They came to bring wisdom and influence,
wit and laughter and social elegance. They came to bring life
to the hallowed halls and colonial-fashioned interiors, luxuriant
with mahogany, marble and heavy gilt-framed paintings – an
environment busy with maids and manservants.

Coralita from the slums walked down the tree-lined avenue
towards the paved courtyards and manicured lawns with
swaying coconut trees. The heady aroma from orchids and
hibiscus wafted across my path as I continued towards the huge
stone steps and the impressive building with more than a dozen
bedrooms. A fairy-tale setting where elegantly dressed guests
drifted across the grounds and through the huge, palatial rooms.
As though I were on an invisible rostrum, my cares were lifted
high above the shabby torments of poverty. I was honoured
and revered – announced by name, shaken firmly by the hand
and presented before the gathering, applauding crowd, with a
clean, new West Indian $20 note for every race I had won at the
pavilion. For much of my life I experienced strife and poverty,
shame and abuse, but today there was a giddy respite.

Ketty was a businesswoman, keeping the scourge of poverty
from our door. When she bought, she expected a swift return.
Besides dealing in fruit and vegetables she visited the quayside
regularly, buying local fish to sell to friends and neighbours.

Ketty also exploited another market when I was sent to buy
bottles of Caribbean rum that were made from the molasses
of Antigua's raw sugar cane. She would pour some into

small glasses and sell the shots to passers-by for a shilling or sixpence. One customer would leave his bicycle outside our home while he sipped his evening tipple. I had never ridden a bicycle before, and the temptation was too great. I secretly rode it over the bridge that spanned the sea, bobbing and weaving along the long, narrow road, before careering into the wall and hitting my chin. I quickly washed the wound in the sea, fearful that Ketty would discover the truth and give me a beating, and returned the bicycle without detection.

Ketty would also drink rum with my stepfather. She married Mac – a huge, bulky man with a ferocious temper, when I was ten. There was no peace when they argued and swore. Their voices grew loud as they stomped around the little house, making idle threats. Mac would snatch at the rum bottle, eager to pour the liquid down his throat, immune to the burning that soaked his gut. He swigged liquor and played cards with his friends through the night. Shunning their raucous humour, I watched their silhouettes in the diffused light until I fell asleep.

Mac was illiterate like his friends. They were stevedores, making a living from unloading the cargo ships at St John's harbour. Every pay day I would visit the quayside, cutting through the throngs of busy travellers and porters, the air thick with oil and steam, to sign for the men's wages and earn a dollar. I would change the English coinage into West Indian dollars and have enough money for five or six square meals. But I preferred to save it, hiding it in the rafters of our house if Ketty did not need food or alcohol.

At 12 years old I joined the Girl Guides. The weekly after-school sessions brought adventure, challenge and a sense of belonging. The sound framework of rules built trust, loyalty, obedience, kindness, purity and courtesy. They helped mould my character and later brought new responsibility as a young leader.

I used the Guide leaders' kitchen, wallowing in pots, pans, marinades and seasonings to achieve my culinary badge. Athletics, needlework, art and craft, domestic skills and hospitality – there were always new triumphs to display on my uniform sleeve.

My mentoring entered a new phase when the Guide commissioner made an announcement.

"There are two places for girls in this unit to attend camp this year. Coralita, you are one of those girls."

Without a penny to my name and no pocket money, finding the long list of essentials that included cutlery and a sleeping bag was impossible, but promised provision came from the Guide leader herself.

Some months later I clambered aboard the bus with the other Guides. It chugged slowly, exhaust streaming and engine bellowing, through the changing geography. Past banana and pineapple plantations and the island's evergreen forest, lurching left and right around the twisting roads that finally ascended to Shirley Heights at the southern tip of the island. At journey's end there was stunned silence. Dozens of eyes stared unblinkingly at the Creator's master palette below the cliffs. The graceful sweeps of both English and Falmouth harbour glinted like sapphires between the volcanic outcrops cloaked in evergreen. Through the shifting shadows long, white ribbons of sand were fringed with palm trees. The views were unrivalled.

Shirley Heights was a former British strategic stronghold, named after the Governor of the Leeward Islands in the eighteenth century. I explored the crumbling relics, treading the worn steps to see the views from the broken down doorways and windows before setting up camp.

There were constant adventures during those raw, exhilarating few days. We rowed to Nelson's Dockyard; swam in the narrow shelved waters; hitched a lift in an American jeep; and came face to face with a donkey who careered through our tent at night. There were spectacular sunsets and campfire vigils beneath a hundred stars as we sang with rousing voices:

"Each campfire lights anew the flame of friendship true; the joy of having known you will last a whole life through." [3]

Chapter 3 **Pathway to the future**

I will lead the blind by ways they have not known, along
unfamiliar paths I will guide them; I will turn the darkness
into light before them and make the rough places smooth.
Isaiah 43: 16 NIV

Mr Hart was a shipping tycoon. He was well-liked by those
around him, often making an impact on their lives, filling them
with a firm resolve to follow where he led. Like most people
on the island, I knew how important he was. I had seen him
on my regular trips to St John's harbour to sign for the men's
wages. Sometimes he circled the quayside, talking business
while mixing with everyone, from reckless sailors to the rich
and influential.

On this occasion he had come to see the headmaster of the
Point Government School with a short and simple offer: he
wanted to offer a poor child a school scholarship. On Mr Hall's
recommendation, he would be my benefactor, not realising
that I was the slip of a lass he saw regularly at the harbour.

I had won the headmaster's attention and respect. Being keen
and bright, I was sent on errands after finishing my class work.
While other pupils were still busy at their desks, I was returning
from the 40-minute round trip to his home to deliver fish or fetch
provisions. I was Mr Hall's first and only choice for the scholarship,
which I clinched easily after sitting the entrance exam.

My uniform was made-to-measure. I went to Emmanuel – the
high-class material shop where I worked on Saturdays – to
buy the fabric by the yard, taking the familiar route from St
John's Cathedral, past the soft drinks factory, police station and
impressive courthouse. Finally, I faced the large store that was

stocked high and wide with bales of fabric – silk, cotton and taffeta, hectic stripes and audacious, floral prints in rainbow shades that came from the far corners of the globe.

Pausing outside, I recalled my first visit to its spacious, airy interior, when I wore a pink-and-white polka-dot dress and my first and only pair of shoes, bought for my elocution competition. Unannounced, I had fixed my eyes determinedly on the elegant woman behind the till and asked for work. Jobs in Antigua were never advertised: you made your own inquiries. Within a few minutes I had left the shop, with the promise of earning five shillings every Saturday.

I believed I could sell anything. Moving my hands deftly among the luxuriant fabrics, removing the bales for customers to inspect, I would appeal to their vanity and their senses. I used charm and a certain perception to win their approval and ensure constant use of the cash register.

Clients came from the smart plantation houses in the provinces, the business fraternity or the ocean ships that docked regularly at St John's harbour. By late spring a steady influx of patrons bought the latest imports for the annual carnival. They would be draped in bright, daring costumes for a riotous summer fiesta spanning culture and class, as they partied and danced to the reggae rhythm and calypso singers to mark the abolition of slavery a century or so before.

Now on the other side of the till, as a customer, I was equally self-assured. I ordered material for a seamstress to make two sets of uniforms to my chosen pattern. Weeks later I was ready for the Tor Memorial High School, wearing a white blouse, green pleated skirt that skimmed the knee, matching tie and straw boater. At fifteen, I was instantly transformed from a teenager in the ghetto to a budding pupil at one of the most prestigious high schools on the island.

With Mr Hart's generosity I entered a doorway of hope. I was encouraged to visit him at home for my ongoing education expenses for books and further uniforms. I looked forward to those visits – to approaching the grand white-boarded house set back from the road in the prosperous neighbourhood, where crimson and violet blooms scented the driveway, and fruit trees of seemingly every kind cast their long, lean shadows.

The house on Newgate Street became familiar; it was the height of luxury, with three sitting rooms and enormous bedrooms with four-poster beds. Upstairs, I would be shown into a bright, airy room – Mr Hart would be at his desk, tapping at the keys of his typewriter with one finger. Greeting me with an engaging smile, he would talk about my progress and settle my school account.

Afterwards I would find Mrs Hart in the kitchen – like her husband she was kind, sensitive and understanding. She would pour me a huge glass of lemonade with a home-made cookie and teach me to use an electric iron. It was a novelty. I usually heated an old heavy iron on an open coal fire outside, wiping the surface meticulously before using a blanket on the ground as a makeshift ironing board.

Every school day I took the steep cliff road above the harbour, watching the cruise liners and fishing boats sailing back and forth between Florida, the Antilles and the other Leeward Islands. Here was, and still is, a tourist paradise, with balmy waters, underwater canyons, schools of squid and colourful, reef fish. It never lost its appeal.

The tropical weather might mean I would leave home in a rain shower but reach school in the sunshine. In September, at the start of the new term, the humidity was stifling. Sweat would build up under my blouse collar. That kind of weather would not subside until Christmas time, when the north-east trade winds across Antigua brought a welcome temperature change.

I walked briskly in the new high-heeled shoes that clanked along the pavement – past the banks, patisserie, chemist, department store and perfumery, entering the school gate from the high street, crossing between the beds of irises and roses and the wide-canopied trees to the main building for older pupils.

The Tor Memorial School was a complete contrast from my last school. Classes were smaller, and teaching was made more effective through advanced facilities. I sat at my own desk and chair among 24 pupils, transfixed at first by the masterpieces that plastered the walls – vivid portraits, landscapes, collages and text with illustrative colour.

But from the outset I knew I was different. A girl from "Poor Point" who had to make do. A girl unaccustomed to outings and treats, pampering and encouragement. Unaccustomed to a soft bed with stories and books, roaming carefree in a large open garden or eating hearty welcoming meals after school. I was different, and I was made to feel it.

There was often a sense of uneasiness and disbelief when I faced the other pupils. It first happened after I was seen by the assistant stevedore's daughter while attending the interview.

"I saw you at my school. Did you come for a servant's job?" she ventured the next day.

Learning the truth – and that I was placed in a higher class than herself – produced open astonishment.

When I reached sixth form, the divide widened. There were just ten pupils at the top of the school and every parent, except mine, had a profession. There was no status expectation when you came from the slums. My academic mind, schooled for the senior Cambridge exams, had put me in a unique position, opening a door of hope for similar future generations. But there was a cost. It meant growing exclusion. Exempt from the privileges and lively social calendar that came with affluence and influence, I became a solitary figure, unable to push past the cultural boundaries. Instead of dancing round the maypole or attending the sixth form finale, I studied and learnt, having sold my books to the lower years so that I could buy new ones to help me move on in my education.

A nurturing hand was held out to me during these years. Miss Loving was loving by name and loving by nature. Her long, thin, caramel-coloured face was lit with smiling, bespectacled eyes. Tall, buxom, with a small, nipped-in waist, she was kind and sensitive.

In the school house we sipped tea from the best bone china. Like a well-meaning aunt, she gave encouragement, counsel and care. It sparked an ongoing friendship and a ready source of help that provided money and advice when I had my first set of bras tailor-made at Jules Superstore in St John's. It also meant shilling loans for school events until I found enough glass bottles to wash and sell.

I was nearing the end of my school life when life itself hung in the balance. There was little warning of the angry torrent that would hit the skies, of the fierce beating winds that would pound Antigua without mercy when the hurricane came. The air was eerie and still. The sun was veiled with scurrying black clouds. There was an evil foreboding that brought thick and impeding gloom.

I was at home as a growing, frenzied panic hit the neighbourhood. There were gnarled and seasoned residents who had seen and read about the past devastation unleashed by hurricanes, and now there was fury in the heavens that was being whipped up and was ready to be unleashed.

The rain started – a quiet patter on the corrugated iron roof as people crammed into our little shack – running, sweating, fearful and shrieking. More and more bodies seemed to fill its tiny dimensions as Ketty too became increasingly terrified. Evelyn and Jackie were no longer at home – only I was left to bring a sense of calm and order as the rain increased and the deluge began, as the wind gathered speed and the shadows darkened.

The noise became deafening. The winds tore incessantly at the slatted shutters, and the rain beat like a thousand drums on the roof. It drove humanity closer, wedged and huddled against the growing ferocity outside. As water seeped in, the house swayed from side to side on its brick-cornered props, and the oil lamps flickered throughout the night. Meanwhile, I sat obediently in the family tin bath as it floated on the rising water. I felt fearless, comforted and warm, praying and knowing that Jesus would take care of us. It was like resting secure under a duvet cover as the storm raged and lashed throughout the long, bellowing night.

By morning all was quiet, but the aftermath was evident. Fruit trees and palm trees had been uprooted, houses had blown down, and sheep, cattle, goats and chickens were dead. We picked our way through the devastation as the island ground to a standstill and the full effects were realised. Schools were closed, supplies cut and transport stopped. It was a day we would never forget.

The Tor Memorial School stood firm and erect like an unscathed warrior against the stormy battle. It continued to serve me well for the remaining few terms of my education, which ended with my senior Cambridge exams and the passport to my future.

I began a secretarial job for two missionaries at the Christian mission. I tapped at the typewriter keys, made the tea and organised appointments. I had a large, fashionable wardrobe with tailored suits, floral dresses and matching shoes that were donated to the mission by wealthy Americans.

The work became the springboard for a life-changing experience after I learned about the crusade meetings at the Pilgrim Holiness Church. They were led by American Billy Graham – a dynamic young man with a warm message that cut across every culture and class. The seven-day event brought people in their droves from across the island's hundred or so square miles. Rich and poor, those with cars and those who walked, they filled the two-storey stadium and overflowed into the street outside, where the preacher's voice was relayed by loudspeaker. The stirring messages never let up. The singing could have raised the roof. There were calls for healing and calls to walk in the light, with the Good Shepherd who holds life. There was wonder and amazement as the lame walked, the blind saw and the deaf heard. It was revolutionary and miraculous.

"Jesus will change your life for ever," proclaimed the besuited speaker.

Charged with emotion, those meetings cut quick to the heart as thousands made a public pledge of trust and faith. They were something completely different.

Tears mingled with joy as an unknown peace and excitement swept through my shaking body. Jesus beckoned me to a new and specific beginning, as his heavenly presence flooded that massed arena. I was 19, and I joined the throngs of people at the front of the stage. My heartfelt sorrow for the past became a clean slate for the future. The promise of strength in weakness, light in darkness and safety in danger came from the Saviour of the world that night when I pledged my all. It meant revival, renewal and refreshment for my whole being. It meant I was never the same again.

I left the Moravian Church to go to the Mission Church, which was more in tune with this kind of experience. Then I saw my former pastor, who had watched over my church attendance since childhood. His eyes were sad and downcast.

"I was thinking of giving you a scholarship to teacher training college, but since you are leaving, I cannot," he said. It was like a cruel stab to my heart, as the Moravian Church ran the only teacher training college in Antigua. If I had known, maybe I would have stayed.

But there was little time to catch my breath, with the whirlwind of activities that followed my Mission Church membership. Everyday was God's day, and church became my life.

"If you take God into your heart, you can take him everywhere you go," was Brother Taylor's stirring message.

So I took him to the weekly Sunday school, Bible study, prayer meetings, choir practice and on to the streets, delivering the good news of Jesus on Saturdays to strangers. There was fire in our souls as Brother Taylor led from the front, speaking from street corners about the God who saves and cares. He brought a sense of unity that wove his flock together like a glorious tapestry. It was powerful. We looked out for one another, shared resources and shone bright in what, at times, could be a dark, forbidding place.

At this time many men and women were rising up and breaking away from the vicious cycle of poverty and destruction. They were grappling with new positions, education and opportunities and challenging the status quo that had kept them tied down since the slave trade, centuries before. But with them came a small minority who rebelled openly against injustice, authority and the ruling classes. This brought fear and sometimes senseless violence – even at the Tor Memorial School, where a pupil had her throat cut, leaving her permanently scarred.

Chapter 4 Eviction and peril

He won't brush aside the bruised and the hurt, and he won't disregard the small and insignificant, but he'll steadily and firmly set things right. He won't tire out and quit, He won't be stopped until he's finished the work – to set things right on earth.
Isaiah 42: 3-4 The Message Bible

There was a sense of pride when the carefully crafted cabinet was put on the wall at Ketty's house, near the bed I inherited after sister Evelyn left home. The cabinet was a further friendship offering from Jim, the boy who walked with me to high school, carrying my books. He had made it himself, adding shelves and a glass door that I locked with a key. It was a labour of love.

Jim was chivalrous, well-meaning and generous. He also wanted to marry me. He bought me meals, gifts and ice cream and cakes from Nooks, in St John's. His skin was like polished ebony, and his liquorice eyes were always merry and dancing. We shared our hearts, and the joys and woes that came our way. Then Jim left – he took a plane to the Virgin Islands, working for a better and easier wage as a trainee architect. After he left, he wrote each week, sending clothes and enclosing money that I would lock in the prized cabinet with the wages from my job.

After returning from church one day, I was aghast to find the cabinet glass door was smashed open. Only a few prized knickknacks remained: the bundle of notes and coins had gone. Mac had stolen the money for gambling.

"Why did you not just ask me, if you wanted money?" I asked.

Mac's incessant voice grew loud, his eyes wide and menacing as I backed away in fear. I knew not to cross him. He was a tall, violent man. When I had done something wrong, he had chased me down, lassoing me with his leather belt and lashing my bare flesh.

"Your father left you no money in his will, so why should I ask you for anything?" he shouted.

"Have you anywhere to live? No. Well get out. Get out of my house. Get out now."

I turned to Ketty in numb disbelief. "Where have I got to go?"

She shrugged her shoulders. "If you have got to go, you have got to go."

With trembling hands, I collected my clothes, mattress and a few cooking utensils and left my mother's house. I had no money and little hope. In just a few minutes, without warning or reason, I was homeless. A huge lump came to my throat, and I sobbed.

I was afraid, confused and shaking uncontrollably. I did not consider the Mission Church as an obvious safe harbour. Only Aunt Violet, one of its members, came to mind. She lived in a large house just yards away. She was like a real mother, kind and compassionate. But asking Aunt Violet for a place to live would have been foolhardy. Her husband was a notorious womaniser, who would watch me from the upstairs veranda of their house when I washed and showered at the standpipe.

Instead, I walked across town to the fine colonial houses twenty minutes away. My footsteps were heavy and weary when I reached Mrs Dutton's home. Her four-bedroom house was set back from the road. Its sunlit veranda overlooked a neatly tended garden with flowering fruit trees, only yards from where Ketty's godmother lived. Her son Richard was born the same day as me. We grew up together in the same run down community until the family became prosperous. They bought a shop, built a small empire and climbed the ladder of wealth, shaking off poverty and embracing fine living, like their relatives who ran a thriving furniture business.

Mrs Dutton opened the door to see me clutching my meagre belongings. She eyed me with suspicion. I was still sobbing. In a faltering voice, I looked into the face of the only woman who could help.

"Mrs Dutton, please let me stay with you. Please let me stay. My Mum and Mac have chucked me out. I have nowhere else to go."

There was a long pause as she stood in the doorway of the large entrance hall, meeting my gaze.

"You are a young woman of vulnerable age," she said. "If anything should happen to you, I would be responsible. I cannot let you stay here."

There was fear in Mrs Dutton's voice, and I understood. Many young girls from the slums became pregnant, bringing disgrace to their families. I had always hoped for a better life with purpose and dignity, but I was too tired and despondent to try to allay her fears.

By now the sun was slipping from the sky as dusk came. Broken-hearted, I trudged back down the path and turned into the main road. News travels fast on the streets in Antigua, and some hours later I heard about a shack to rent near Poor Point. It was tiny – not big enough to keep a car. It housed a bed, table and gas stove, and I hung my clothes from nails on the wall.

I settled down to sleep on the mattress that night. It was bleak and unfamiliar. A tight pain gripped my stomach. The memories of the day roamed my mind like dark, terrifying intruders. There was no peace. I was rejected, alone and desperate for an answer to life's problems.

The little slum house near the beach became my shelter for the next three years. The grim recollections lessened as the days became brighter. I earned extra money with home-tutoring, labouring long and hard after work to teach a group of illiterate young men from the Seventh Day Adventist Church. I heard about their plight while working at the mission. They were attentive and enthusiastic, learning to read and write with relative ease. It opened the gateway to their future – one became a preacher, another a university graduate and a third a businessman in England – and also unlocked a door for me. They alerted me to a new teaching post at the Goodwill Academy. I applied for the job through the headmaster, who knew my adult pupils from church. Without a formal application, interview or teaching qualification, I began the job the next day, using my senior Cambridge qualification to prove I was proficient at arithmetic, English, geography, history, French and health science.

It was a cloudless, sunny day, and I took a sharp intake of breathe on entering the school hall at the Goodwill Academy. Wearing a simple floral dress, best high-heeled shoes and clutching a brown leather briefcase, I arrived before nine in the morning after a brisk 30- minute walk. I was just 21 – the youngest teacher, from the poorest area, mixing with seasoned professionals. Only the hand of God could have provided such a breakthrough.

Teaching became my vocation. It provided joy and satisfaction, as the tools of knowledge rested easily in my hands. I became determined and focused during the six-hour day at the fee-paying establishment for 300 pupils. Life and creativity were the hallmark of lessons for the 40 ten- and eleven-year-olds. Their young, fertile minds absorbed knowledge like blotting paper, whether it was Shakespeare's sonnets, the geography of the Himalayas or British politics. There were no hidden formulas, just a God-given inspiration that turned the cogs of understanding in their young minds.

Teaching was a paintbrush to colour the minds of a new generation. I drew from my own reservoir of wisdom, gained at school and from years of reading. It opened the annals of learning to give fresh empowerment. It came without difficulty or toil. I used a new, radical approach to overturn the brutal methods I had endured as a schoolgirl. I was patient and kind but also firm, emphasising the motto: "Learn all you can, and can all you learn – to be the happiest class in the school." I won the esteem of teachers, pupils and parents alike.

The school was popular with the middle-classes. It attracted a wide selection of pupils who were always courteous, attentive and respectful. There was also honesty and humour in the classroom. During morning and afternoon prayers young Simon remembered my instructions to pray at home. A long request was sent heavenward on Friday night. On Saturday and Sunday, kneeling before his bed, he simply said: "The same as last night, Jesus."

Joan Armatrading had a bright future as a well-known singer and songwriter. As a small child she would make her way from Poor Point to the school where I taught. She was seven years old and in the class below mine. I knew her as a baby; we developed a strong friendship among the shabby homesteads and poverty. She was pretty and bright, with long straight hair. The apple of her mother's eye, she always wore fine, well-pressed clothes. Even at a tender age she had a voice with perfect pitch. Eventually as a young woman her huge, raw vocals brought her international stardom, which continued for many, many years. While Joan's future would beckon in the UK, mine was about to be seriously threatened by a secret, horrifying terror that would continue for the next three decades.

It was a typical Saturday, and I was giving out gospel tracts in the afternoon. The sultry temperatures had gone, and it was wintertime, just weeks before Christmas. The sun was still warm, and St John's was busy with traders, tourists, cyclists and shoppers. It was business as usual – fresh fruit and vegetables spilled onto the pavement beneath rusting, corrugated roofs.

Women with headscarves and men in short-sleeved shirts, some wearing panamas, walked by when Royston approached. He was a confident young man of mixed race. He shot me a long, determined gaze and took the tract I offered, eager to hear about the church mission meetings.

His response caught me unaware. "I will come to church with you on Sunday," he told me boldly. "But I am coming to get you."

"I beg your pardon."

He continued: "I am coming to get you, because I am going to marry you."

I ignored the menacing overtones, speaking instead about the forthcoming Wednesday prayer meeting. Royston crooked his head towards me. "I will walk you to the prayer meeting, and we will go together," he insisted.

I grew up in a community that never locked their doors. Familiarity brought an unwritten code of trust that was rarely breached. Four days later Royston walked through the entrance of my little shack. He was uninvited. He was unexpected. He tracked me down easily after making inquiries in the tight-knit neighbourhood.

It was December 5, 1955, and dark and cold outside. I reached for my coat, ready to leave for the Mission Church, when Royston stretched across me and clasped a firm hand round my wrist.

Sensing danger, I protested. "I thought we were going to church."

He grew angry. "No, you are not going."

"What do you mean?"

Frenzied with rage, he threw me on the bed. He started to undress me. I wrestled with him. I crossed my legs tightly. I screamed. I cried for help. But he was strong – much stronger than me. When he left, I was utterly disgusted. Numb. Terrified. Ashamed. I had been defiled. I had wanted to remain a virgin, keeping myself for the right man on my wedding night.

Day or night he came to my home. Seven days a week, twice on Sundays, he repeatedly raped me. I told no-one. It remained an awful secret for 43 years. It continued for months until I was pregnant.

I grew to hate Royston. He was wicked and deceitful. He insisted on attending Sunday church services and prayer meetings. He made a personal declaration of faith before the whole congregation. He told everyone we were dating, and he would marry me.

Royston's reputation soon became evident. He had been to prison twice. He was known as a violent thief with few morals. Brother Taylor, the pastor, took me aside one day.

"If the Lord had called you to work in Africa, as a missionary among all the turmoil, you would go and sacrifice your life. But this is worse. You are sacrificing your life by going out with this man."

I could not have an abortion like many of the slum girls. It went against all my godly principles. Once I found a dead baby on the beach. It came from a back-street abortion clinic where girls as young as 13 had ended their pregnancies.

My job hung in the balance. As a single mother I would lose my standing in the community and be unable to teach. I believed I had no alternative. I was forced into a loveless marriage to safeguard my vocation.

The wedding was the worst day of my life. It heralded torment and hell. I did not want any reminders – the only photographs taken were sent to Royston's brother in America. The wedding dress was secondhand. It was beautiful and came from America.

The simple ceremony was held at a church in the country. The car that called for me circled the building time and again, because Royston was late. Almost half the invited guests boycotted the event. Those from the little Mission Church turned their back on me, making a stand against my decision to marry a notorious criminal. I was no longer allowed to serve in the church that had been my life for the last three years. Only Aunt Violet and Marge Armatrading and her daughter Joan continued to support me.

I suffered contempt on the streets: "You have married this man, and you are still holding your head up high as if nothing has happened." There was humiliation in the classroom: "Did you know that her husband is a thief, who has been in prison?" It cut deep, but I knew I was blameless.

I continued to teach at the Goodwill Academy and rented a two-bedroom house in a better neighbourhood, ready for the new arrival. There was a dining room, outside kitchen and shutters between the sitting room and main bedroom. Royston was a carpenter. He made a settee, rocking chair, dining room table and a larder cupboard for the kitchen. The garden was shaded by banana, coconut, sugar apple and soursop trees. I grew tomatoes and spinach and swam and fished in the sea nearby. It was the perfect environment for a growing child.

I would turn left out of the front gate to fetch water from the standpipe that was five minutes' walk away. A huge metal drum, with a sieve to catch the debris, was used to recycle the winter rainfall. There was a tin bath beneath the soursop tree, but I was always wary of Mr Newton, who was a peeping tom.

I did not stop teaching until seven days before Kevin was born, and returned to the school seven days later. That was the custom in the Caribbean. After six hours of labour, baby Kevin made his debut at St John's Hospital. He was born white, because Royston was of mixed parentage – his mother was black and his father was white. Kevin's skin turned darker over the ensuing months, and darker still in the burnished sun.

I cradled the little bundle in my arms. There were mixed emotions for the baby who had changed my fortunes. It brought sadness and a heavy heart. I paid my godmother, Agatha, to care for Kevin while I resumed work. She also did the washing and cleaning; so I only had to cook and shop.

Royston was jealous of the baby. There were angry outbursts and constant demands. He continued to rape me, using threats and beatings. It became an evening or daily ritual. I was afraid and unloved, as he sought tighter controls on my life.

He would look at me and snarl: "So you think you are a pearl of great price?"

I kept silent in case I was beaten again. I visited Ketty with a cry for help.

"Royston is cruel and violent. What do I do?"

Ketty was pouring out tots of rum for visiting clients. She looked at me with intense brown eyes. "Leave your father and mother and cleave to your husband," she said, without an ounce of pity.

Royston did not have regular work. I gave him money or he helped himself from my purse to subsidise his wages. He wanted to replace his radio, so I obligingly bought him a bigger one. The following week he blatantly took a similar model from the shop in town. That brought Royston his third prison sentence – three and a half years.

I wrote regularly, enclosing money for an electrical apprenticeship while he served time. There were threats if

I did not visit. I took the bus to the other side of the island, near the pavilion, pacing the prison's grim perimeters before finally summoning courage to enter. The prison officer always gave us private time together. Royston would drag me into the toilets and rape me. There were never any contraceptives in those days, so before long I was carrying his second child.

My sister contacted Royston while he was behind bars. She sowed seeds of doubt in his suspicious mind, implying that there was something underhand about the long-standing tutoring arrangement with the Seventh Day Adventist Church members. Royston was simmering with rage by my next visit. He knew the men visited our home for weekly lessons, and that I helped supply the text books and writing paper. There were long interrogations and spiteful jibes.

"So you have been having a good time while I am away."

I looked him straight in the eye. The money helped bridge the shortfall in my teacher's wage. There was no basis for any sinister allegations. "What do you think I would do?" I demanded. "Am I likely to lock myself away like you?"

There was no warning. Royston slapped me hard across the face. It left a red, stinging mark.

When Royston left prison, he did odd carpentry jobs at the airbase. He gained access to the American residential quarters, and his light-fingered ways continued when he took their clothes and money. I persuaded Royston to escape to England. I wanted to keep him out of trouble – and out of my life.

By this time I was teaching at the Hall Secondary School – a private school run by my former headmaster, who had recommended me for the school scholarship when I was a teenager. Mr Hall was still a commanding character. His loud bark had not lessened over the years; so I was careful not to cross him. But there was a compassionate side to his nature. He lent me £5 for Royston's passage to London, and I repaid the regular monthly instalments from my wages.

My husband promised to send me money, but none arrived. Instead there were threatening letters, insisting I joined him with the children. At first I ignored them, basking in the peace and pleasure that came with growing independence.

Teaching continued to be rewarding and sustained my growing family, that now totalled two boys and a girl. I wore a green uniform like the pupils and taught French and health science, since I achieved credits in these subjects at school. Many of the youngsters came from affluent, upwardly mobile families, travelling by car or bus from the outlying countryside. They often brought weekly gifts of mangoes, pineapples or vegetables. Their parents were eager for them to benefit from a fresh, exciting input. It gave me free rein. Lessons full of fun and invention often spilled out into my back yard after school.

When youngsters celebrated a birthday, there were class donations of flour, eggs, sugar and butter. Fifty children would cram into my garden in the late afternoon to help make the customary birthday cake, baked in an outside oven over hot coals and eaten beneath the shady coconut tree. The oven was a crude, shelved box that I made from metal oddments, but the cake was delicious.

Blueprints for lives were often drawn in the classroom. My teaching experience brought a perception that often pinpointed the potential of future doctors, lawyers, sportsmen – and even criminals.

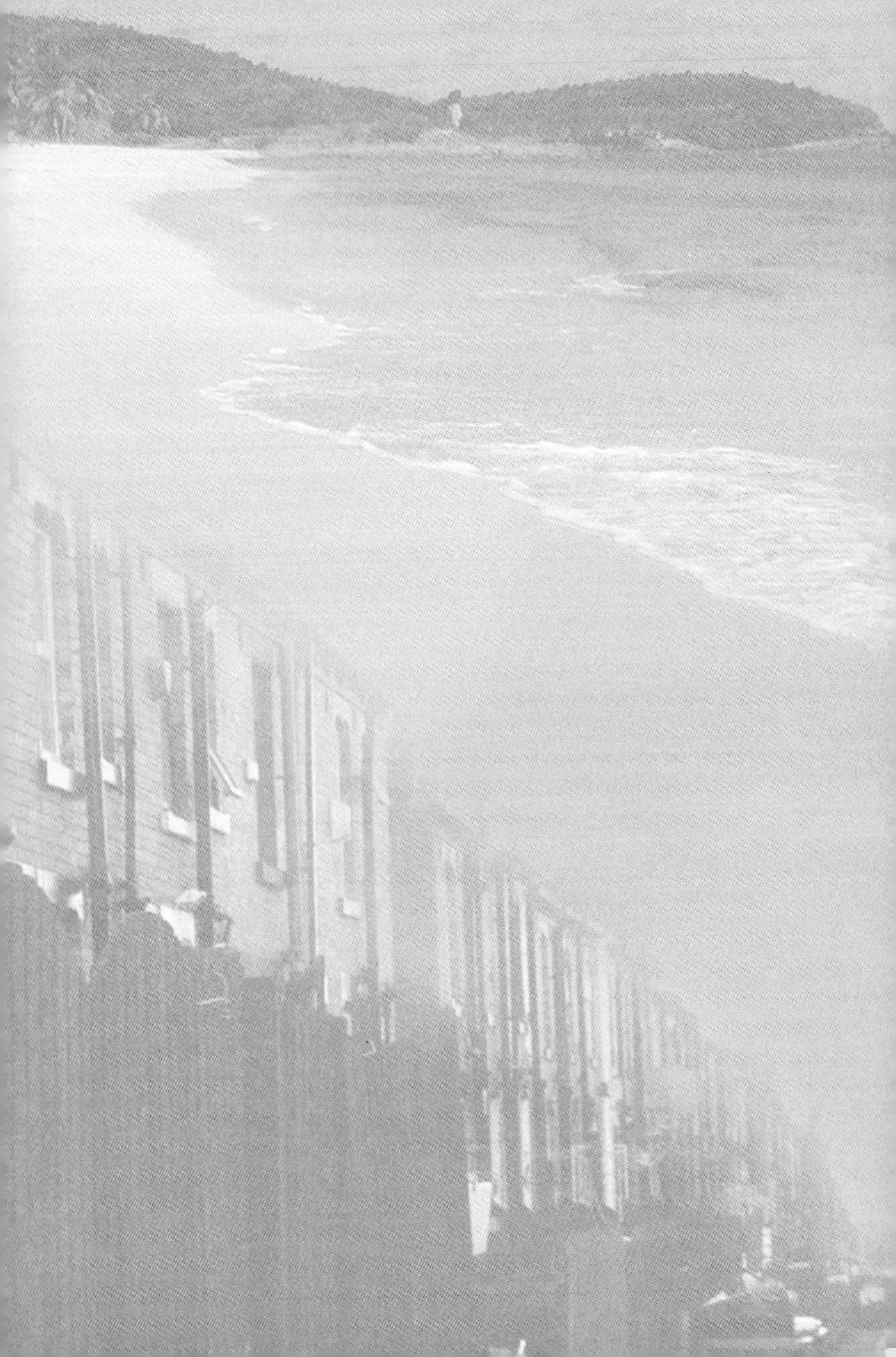

Chapter 5 Passage to England

*Before even time began my life was in his hand. He knows
my name, he knows my every thought, he sees each tear
that falls and hears me when I call . . . He'll never leave me,
no matter where I go.* Tommy Walker [4]

The Ascania was bleached white in the dazzling sunlight. The
700-passenger ship grew in size as our speedboat approached.
It was the end of November 1960, and my life was about to
move into uncharted waters.

Kevin, Sarah and Gavin – my three small children under four
years old – clasped the hem of my summer dress as the
speedboat soared and plunged through the waves. Then it
circled the massive steamer and rested against the port side so
that we could board.

Early that morning, in the waking dawn, we had left our familiar
little house. Grasping a single worn suitcase and my passport,
we waved goodbye to Aunt Agatha and dozens of cheering
schoolchildren. It was barely six months since Royston had
left for England. They had passed in a happy blur until his
letters arrived. They were short and frequent: the sprawling
handwriting conveyed a simple, terrifying message. Unless
I joined him immediately with the children, he would kill me.
I sold my furniture and the dinner service that was a wedding
gift to help finance the £80 one-way ticket to England. The
financial shortfall was met by Mr Hart.

Royston promised a fine house and untold opportunities, but
nothing could compensate for leaving the island that was
my home – an island rich in beauty and simplicity. Pain and
nostalgia wrenched at my heart that day as the boat sailed

out of St John's harbour towards the man I hated and feared. Towards a life of impending doom and hardship.

We left the string of Caribbean Islands for the ten-day voyage to Southampton on the English south coast. The tropical azure waters turned murky grey, and the sky lost its summer haze as we reached the Atlantic Ocean and headed north-east towards Europe.

The Ascania was a busy floating community of native West Indians from Tobago, Trinidad, Jamaica, Barbados and Antigua who were about to seek their fortune in the UK. They filed along the unending corridors, ate in the gigantic cafeteria and slept in the narrow cabins that criss-crossed beneath the decks.

I was nervous and naïve. At 25 years old I had never left the familiar shores of Antigua – a recognised backwater with no trains or fast, sophisticated cars like its larger, established Caribbean neighbours. An easy banter existed between the Jamaicans, who were quick to help me with the children.

Four days into the voyage, the sky was heavy and threatening in the Arctic temperatures as November turned to December. The ship reached its optimum speed. Ferocious waves poured across the decks. The ship lurched back and forth in the gigantic headwinds. The turbulence increased, and passengers were seasick. Nausea swept across us like a plague as the horizon dipped dramatically.

Mrs Jarvis, my next-door neighbour, was a welcome, familiar figure. We clutched each other for support with the children as the boat shifted and surged through the swelling waters. Together we went below decks to escape the icy gusts, but then we were terrorised by two crew members, who tried to molest us in our cabins. Screaming, we threatened to report them to the captain. They backed away, but we did not rest until we reached dry land.

My stomach continued to turn over. I was desperate and afraid of the unknown future, but I needed to be strong for the children. Every secure and faithful prop had been removed, but my faith in God did not falter. Though pressed by many a foe, I prayed that I would not tremble on the brink of poverty or woe.

We docked at Southampton on December 6. The night air was biting and cold. Wearing scanty summer clothes and holding hands, the children and I descended the gangplank to frenzied activity. Passengers, sailors and porters with luggage swarmed like bees beneath the neon-lit sky.

Royston jostled through the crowds towards us, his eyes steady and unblinking. It was a sombre, cold-hearted meeting.

"Did you bring the rum?" he demanded, without looking at the children.

The evening was veiled in cigarette smoke. We walked quickly to keep warm, but my feet were like blocks of ice. Trailing closely behind Royston's massive frame, we headed for the car park, where his friend would be our chauffeur. Silently, we slid into the back seats for the four-hour drive along the fast open roads to London and through the industrial smog to the slumbering streets of Stoke Newington.

We drew up outside a two-storey turn-of-the-century property, and Royston showed us to the top-floor tenement. Our new home, with an outside toilet, was one squalid room. We would eat, sleep and wash within its stark grey walls. There was a small paraffin heater, a double bed with a filthy mattress and a sink with cold water that made me yelp.

Royston was joined by his friends – boisterous, hostile and swigging rum until they left, after midnight. Finally, exhausted from my husband's sexual desires, I slept until the early morning while the children huddled together in a makeshift bed on the floor. So began my shocking journey into a foreign world. It was far removed from Antigua and Royston's promises of prosperity.

With a warm secondhand coat and boots, I was sent out to buy provisions. Car and factory fumes clung to the stale, polluted air. Rows of back-to-back Victorian houses with grimy facades and crumbling brickwork backed on to small yards. I paced the seemingly endless pavements to the market in Dalston, three miles away.

I asked countless times for directions, but found them difficult to follow. Turning continually left and right, and left again, crossing the maze of drab grey streets, I soon got lost. Staring at a sea of different-coloured faces, bleak and unsmiling, I passed strange pawn shops, launderettes and corner grocery stores. The winter temperatures were merciless. My aching feet were frozen with chilblains; so I bought a threepenny bus ticket for the journey home. That journey opened my eyes to unexpected racial prejudice.

Two Jamaican women looked at me as I walked past them down the aisle of the moving bus. There was an immediate outcry: "Look how she black. She black, black, black," said one to the other.

"She from Africa, that why she so black," came the reply.

The conversation continued. "Perhaps she can understand what we are saying."

"No, those Africans cannot speak English. They do not understand."

I sat in silence until I left the bus. Facing them both, I announced: "Excuse me, would you mind moving out of the way?"

"Oh gracious me," shouted one of them, "she speaks English."

More feelings of isolation were to follow a few days later. It was my first Sunday in England, and I heard a church band outside the front door. I followed the procession with the children, eager to go to church but it was a long walk to the other side of the community. We sat at the back, the only black faces in the hundred-strong congregation. No-one spoke to us. We left just as we arrived, friendless and lonely. I cried all the way home. If this was English Christianity, I did not want to know any more. Royston had removed my Bible, and I was not allowed to talk about God or Jesus. I remembered my memory verses from old, sang the rousing hymns I had learnt in Antigua and watched Sunday morning worship on Royston's new television when he was not in the house.

We lived on the breadline despite the family allowance income to subsidise his shop-fitter earnings. I knew how to be resourceful. We tightened our belts, with secondhand clothes and a carbohydrate diet devoid of expensive imported fruit and vegetables. We ate cereal, rice, potatoes and toad-in-the-hole. Stew was made from boiled meat bones from the butcher, and coley was fried or baked and mashed with butter or salt. We shared the kitchen with the couple downstairs. I fed the gas meter with sixpences to cook, clean and wash with hot water, but the money was often stolen from the meter. We walked to the local swimming baths for a shower, because there was no bathroom.

Then I became pregnant again. "It is all your fault. You should not have allowed it to happen," bawled Royston. "You cannot have the baby. You will have to have an abortion."

I protested: "I do not know where to go."

"I know someone who will give you something to get rid of it," he said.

One night he brought me a quarter of a bottle of vodka with black pepper. Too afraid to argue, I drank it and was promptly sick. Nothing happened. The pregnancy continued, despite other potions administered in a bizarre bid to get rid of the baby.

Nine months after my arrival in England, Lee was born, in September. He needed an operation to correct a malformed eye he had when he was born, perhaps as a result of the weird potions I took.

Lee became an immediate target for his father's contempt and insults.

"He stinks. Get him out of here!" he shouted.

Like a ferocious lion, Royston's angry roars continued. While he favoured Gavin, buying him a bicycle despite the empty kitty, he turned defiantly against his youngest son, blaming him for my inability to work and ease the finances. He vented his rage against me, hurling slander and slaps in every direction as he continued to rape me every night. I was black and blue. My confidence disappeared; I was unable to look in the mirror. There was nowhere to escape.

"You are ugly and fat," he bellowed. "I do not know what I saw in you."

A year later I was pregnant again, and Royston fell in love with Josie.

"I don't love you, you black old thing," he shouted.

Royston dressed smartly. He bought new clothes and ate at fine restaurants to charm his new and slender young girlfriend. At home his seething temper persisted. His angry outbursts were unprovoked, but his eyes grew dark and sinister. I was walking on the edge of a dangerous precipice that threatened to collapse.

He made constant threats. "You and the children have to get out. I do not want you here any more."

Finally, I was thrown out of the room, with nowhere to go. There were whimpers and protests from the children, who stayed behind as I gathered up my handful of belongings, buttoned my coat and left. On the narrow stone staircase near the front door, I sat down and sobbed. Tears like raindrops fell in huge puddles on the concrete step.

It had been the worst year of my life. Depression had covered me like a shroud. I had lost my appetite and my energy. Countless tears had stung my eyes. I was six months pregnant and the mother of four small children. I was also homeless. Frightened and bewildered, I sobbed for hours. Leaning against the metal railings, I slept. Numb and lifeless, I woke five hours later. The dawn light seeped under the door in the hall. There was the constant hum of traffic.

I had to hatch a new survival plan. I bought a small paraffin heater for the stairs, where I slept fitfully for the next few nights. I pounded the streets by day, walking miles, searching, inquiring, for somewhere to live. Everywhere I went it was the same. "No blacks. No children."

Desperate for advice, I visited the kind Jewish family who ran the nearby corner store. Their personal service and deliveries were widely known, as were their cold meats, vegetables, olives and yeast-free bread – thin, crisp wafers for the Jewish Sabbath and Passover. It was definitely kosher!

Stella was wiping down the counter. She stepped back and gave it a critical look as I entered the familiar surroundings. She smiled. "What can I do for you, Coralita?"

There were few words to retell the terrible saga. "I have got to leave. My husband wants me out. I have nowhere to go."

Stella was astonished. Her compassionate, wide eyes opened even wider. She thought for a minute before answering: "Go to the police station. Tell them you have nowhere to live, and they will take you to a hostel in a black limousine."

Following her advice, I made a personal visit that afternoon. Returning home, I packed my bag and waited. When the two police officers arrived at Oldfield Road, I followed them into the small, decrepit room overrun with dirty washing and dishes in my absence.

Turning to Royston, they said: "What do you have to say about the children?"

"I don't want them," muttered Royston. He gave me a scornful look. "Let her take them."

Chapter 6 **Hostels, hovels and havens**

***He hideth my soul in the cleft of the rock, where rivers of
pleasure I see. He hideth my life in the depths of his love,
and covers me there with His hand.*** *Fanny Crosby* [5]

I spent my birthday at Mornington Lodge, a bleak and
impersonal hostel with four giant dormitories, communal
bathrooms and a large canteen. It provided shelter, protection
and three square meals a day for homeless women and their
children, who were often abused and defenceless.

I made up five beds and tucked up the children the night we
arrived. I saw matron and was added to the chore rota and given
the daily task of cleaning the toilets. It had been a harrowing day.
I was about to retire when a torrent of abuse came from a white
man who crossed my path while visiting his wife.

"You blacks," he snarled. "You are not satisfied with taking our
homes; now you take our hostels."

Dazed, I removed my coat, and he saw I was pregnant. There
was a half-hearted apology. "Sorry, I did not know you were
that way."

The routine at the hostel began at 7.30 each morning. On
waking, I queued for cups of tea and scrambled egg, but the
bread was often stale: I removed the green mould before
giving it to the children. I washed our clothes by hand in the
busy washroom and hung them in the outside yard to dry
– but without a watchful eye, they were liable to be stolen.

A growing influx of nationalities sought sanctuary at Mornington
Lodge. Asians, Chinese, Africans, West Indians and British lived
within close proximity. It often sparked differences and racism.

It was early morning the day after I arrived. I was busy cleaning the toilets.

"What did you do before you came in here?" asked a dusky Jamaican woman.

I looked up momentarily: "In Antigua, where I come from, I used to teach."

"You a teacher," she ridiculed. "I can't believe it."

"Yes," I insisted. "And one of these days I am going to get back my teacher's job."

I turned my strong hands to whatever I was asked to do. Within weeks I was promoted to cleaning the stairs, but I missed my footing on the concrete steps and fell head-over-heels to the bottom of the flight. I was taken to hospital by ambulance – but later discharged with just a few bruises.

Weeks later all four children caught salmonella food poisoning. Sick and feverish, they lost their appetites and grew pale and listless, with sunken heavy eyes. They were isolated at three different hospitals for months as they fought to survive. I caught daily buses to the far reaches of north and central London and the East End to visit them. Heartbroken and exhausted, I watched and waited, praying for their recovery while returning late to the hostel for meals and chores.

By late summer we moved to Ludlow Lodge, near Baker Street. The hostel was a short stroll from the imposing Regency houses that lined the streets near Regent's Park Zoo. The pavements were cleaner, the air fresher, as autumn came and the emerald leaves turned copper and gold. But the residents were noisy, and an encounter with one in particular sparked a clash with the police.

Betty's shouting had been incessant. It reached a deafening crescendo.

Exasperated, I said: "Would you be quiet, please."

Betty was indignant. "Shut up!" she yelled, landing a vicious hand across my face.

I lost my cool. Furious, I picked up a glass and hit her. Betty called the police, who took down her strong allegations in a statement. She insisted the case was heard at court. Three months later the solicitor read my notes at the hearing, where I was cross-examined. There was no case to answer.

Warrington Building at Bethnal Green was old and crumbling. It was neither a hostel nor my own home, but a "halfway" house on a busy main road, near Brick Lane. It was early winter, and Matthew, my fifth child, was just two months old when we first climbed the endless stairs to our new top-floor accommodation. It was grimy and small, with one bedroom and no bathroom.

Bethnal Green, in London's East End, was the centre of the rag trade in the "swinging sixties". An emerging era of bell-bottom trousers, mini-skirts and colourful geometric prints, with trendy precision haircuts and knee-high boots. An era where Jewish and Asian couture mingled with colourful markets, Beatles vocals and Mary Quant make-up. It made astounding fashion sense for a young woman from a Caribbean Mission Church where arms were covered and hats and thick stockings had to be worn, even in the sweltering heat.

It was the winter of 1962-63, the coldest in Britain for over 200 years, when we moved. There were blizzards, heavy frosts and a thick blanket of snow across much of the British Isles for three months. Villages were cut off, power lines were brought down, trains were cancelled and livestock died. In London it was a similar story. Schools, offices and factories closed and traffic was at a standstill, with twelve inches of drifting snow and thick 'pea soup' fogs.

The sub-zero temperatures sent cold shivers through my body. The arctic winds rattled down the narrow East End streets. I was unable to see even one step ahead in the freezing fogs that clung to the cold night air. Petrified, I held on to the lamp-posts and railings, edging slowly and deliberately along the roads with a string of children behind.

With fumbling fingers I cleaned out the grate and made up the coal fire every morning, using rolled newspaper. I hung the washing over the fireguard to dry. I heated the water to wash the children, two at a time, in a tin bath by the fire and dried them as they stood on the dining table. I climbed up and down 60 stairs, with a pram and umpteen youngsters, to shop and hang out the washing on a gigantic, pulley system in the back yard when the weather was fine.

I was glad of Hannelore's help. The German nurse, who lived near the Mildmay Hospital, helped heave the pram up and down stairs. She fetched, carried, washed, cleaned and ironed. She made huge helpings of creamy mashed potato and glasses of punch with Guinness, vanilla and eggs when we were ill.

"As are your days, so will be your strength," said Hannelore, whose strong faith in God burnt in the kiln of kindness.

The dank air, polluted by exhaust fumes and factory waste, made Matthew ill. At six months old, his tiny lungs were congested and his breathing was laboured. He writhed in discomfort, wheezing and coughing throughout the night. He was rushed to hospital with bronchitis and asthma and was sent to St Helen's Convalescent Home in Hertfordshire to recover for six months. I took the train to Welwyn Garden City for weekly visits. The new satellite town was built to ease the poor and overcrowded living conditions in London. Renowned for wide open spaces and modern, expanding facilities in health care, industry, leisure and living, it provided a balance between conservation and development.

I met Phyllis on one of my regular excursions into the countryside to visit Matthew. She was a middle-aged freelance writer, and her daughter was a teacher. She poured out her story of woe during our first meeting. Her children had left home and her husband was a successful businessman who left her for his secretary. She had moved out of their plush family house to a caravan close to Pinewood Film Studios. Phyllis and I became friends. I would visit her mobile home, with its space-saving, collapsing bed and neat galley kitchen. We walked the country lanes and wrote to one another. There were long, honest exchanges over cups of tea and cake. Phyllis would baby-sit and bring presents when she visited us in London. Before Christmas her son arrived on the doorstep with an iced cake and £7 – gifts from Phyllis.

Within months of moving, Royston arrived at the front door with a suitcase. He pushed me aside.

"I have come back," he announced, settling himself by the fire.

Fear gripped the inside of my stomach. I had narrowly escaped detection months previously when he called at Ludlow Lodge, claiming to be my brother. Seeing him at the outside gate I deliberately avoided a meeting, but now his demands, abuse and cruelty had returned with a vengeance. Despite his re-appearance, Royston continued gallivanting. He slept with other women while he lashed out at me. His sexual advances persisted. He became mean and angry if I did not yield.

The daily regime was weary and back-breaking. I did a cleaning job, rising at five in the morning and returning by 6.30 while the children were asleep. Life was hard, money was short, and my health became a casualty. The children were taken into care six times during my frequent hospital stays for childbirth, stress and two operations. I also suffered from a painful, terrifying infection. Thirty years later, I learnt that it was a serious sexual disease resulting from Royston's promiscuity.

One hospital stay, however, provided a new golden opportunity. Denise was in the bed next to mine. She was white, well-educated, with an upper-crust accent. She had never spoken to a black person before, but an unexpected chemistry grew between us. Against every cultural protocol, she extended a large warm hand and clutched me to her motherly bosom like a lost child.

Denise was kind and caring, going the extra mile to prove her worth. Her commitment and goodness would lock us together in a tight, sustaining friendship that was forged in my own deep waters of pain and adversity.

Our light-hearted banter broke the austere atmosphere at the London Hospital in Whitechapel. "One of these days I am going to have a nice a big house with toilets in every room," said Denise, queuing for the communal bathroom.

Not to be outdone, I added: "And one of these days, I am going back to Antigua."

After my hospital discharge, a letter arrived on the doormat. It was written in neat, legible handwriting:

My dear Corally,

It was such a pleasure talking to you in hospital. I would very much like to pursue our friendship, and if you agree, please would you write to me at the enclosed address.

With love from Denise.

Within a week Denise was standing outside the front door. By now she had swapped her hospital nightdress for a smart, grey suit to resume her housing manager's job with Islington Council. She made the detour after work to visit with fruit for the children.

In the tiny kitchen, surrounded by my flock of inquisitive offspring, she insisted that I attend an urgent hospital appointment while she baby-sat. Within minutes she was elbow-deep in suds, helping to wash a stack of dishes after ushering me out of the door. On my return there was a large spread on the table, and the kettle was boiling. So began a friendship which continues to bloom 50 years later.

Her father was a butcher. She lived in a beautiful house in Bethnal Green. Sometimes we would visit, sitting down to a meal or sipping tea in the former parlour that was a sitting room. Denise trod a well-worn path to our door, appearing at least twice a week with fruit, cake and clothes she had made for the children. She showed me the changing face of England and the real East End.

There were trips to pie-and-mash shops to sample jellied eels. We travelled to deepest Kent in her little bubble car, exploring the "garden of England" with its gently rolling countryside, weather-boarded cottages and peculiar oast houses. Nearer home, we went to the Good Shepherd Church, where the children attended Sunday school. We visited Victoria Park, where countless varieties of oaks, horse-chestnuts, hawthorn and pink-flowering cherry trees grew beside ornamental lakes and children's playgrounds – where roaming deer and floral havens graced the gated acres between Tower Hamlets and Hackney. There were many outings, but one was unsurpassed.

"I want to take you somewhere special," said Denise one afternoon, leading me upstairs to her vast wardrobe.

Opening the sliding mirrored doors, she thumbed through the various outfits. She was undecided.

"You will need something distinctive," she said. "Why don't you choose?"

Scanning the long rail, I pulled out a black velvet suit with tassels and a neatly tailored jacket. It was a perfect fit for the forthcoming event.

Cleopatra, starring Elizabeth Taylor and her future husband, Richard Burton, was hitting the review columns when we took the train to the West End. We joined the throngs of cinemagoers at Leicester Square as the bright neon lights flickered and glared against the inky sky. Caught under the spell of 20th Century Fox, we watched the lavish, money-busting epic in the circle seats while munching a huge box of chocolates. We celebrated further at London's prestigious five-star Savoy Hotel in The Strand, passing the uniformed doorman, through the opulent art-deco entrance to the restaurant, with its panoramic views across the Thames. It was the grandest feast imaginable. That unforgettable night cost Denise half her monthly wage. It was divine inspiration to help ease the pressure of life in the East End.

She was one of the few people who took Royston to task. Her fierce tongue and unflinching courage instantly subdued the man of steel. When there was no money to buy the boys' trousers, Denise noticed the huge rolls of fabric from the market that Royston had stashed away to sell for a future profit. She moved the material between her thumb and forefinger.

 "It's good material. This will be perfect for the boys' trousers." She bundled the roll under her arm and left, returning a few days later with four new, neatly pressed garments.

"What happened to the material?" asked Royston, when we sat together later that afternoon.

"I took it for the boys," said Denise. "They needed new trousers, so I made them for all of them."

Another time there was an unexpected visitor. Sarah answered the door and showed her into the room, announcing: "Mum, one of Dad's girlfriends is here."

There was no time to answer before Denise rose to her feet. Red-faced and furious, she turned on the girl. "What are you doing here? Get out. How dare you come into this house to ask for these children's Dad? Get out now."

Josie left immediately. Shortly afterwards, Royston returned.

"Your girlfriend is waiting downstairs. I told her to leave," snapped Denise. "You can get out too."

When I was badly beaten, the children telephoned Denise. She came as soon as she could, bathing and dressing the wounds and vowing vengeance.

I tried to stem the growing family. I went to a family planning clinic for contraceptives, but Royston discarded them in disgust. Josie became the mother of Royston's child while I was pregnant again, with twins. She rang, explaining that she wanted to marry Royston. I was quick to respond: "You can have him, dear. I am happy to get a divorce."

Royston did not press for a divorce, but his attentions were firmly fixed on his new family. Without warning, he ransacked my cupboards, taking pots, pans and bed linen to set up home with Josie.

There was another strong alliance in the fight against poverty and despair. Sylvia and I met at Warrington Building, but she moved to the downstairs flat shortly after I arrived. Sylvia came from the Caribbean. She was a grafter who knew every trick in the book when it came to survival. She had a huge, infectious personality and a beaming smile across her broad native features. Her husband was a gambler; his constant habit put the rent in arrears and there was often no money for food or electricity. We shared resources, ideas and a growing understanding that was forged over a shared glass of ale in the local pub – and when I helped deliver her baby.

It was almost ten at night when her husband knocked at my door in the depths of winter. "Please come quickly," he stammered. Sylvia was having frequent, painful contractions when I arrived in the pitch black. The electricity board had cut off the power because the bill was unpaid. We had to light the room with candles before I could deliver the infant – a healthy baby girl who Sylvia named Carol – similar to Coral – in remembrance of me.

We took it in turns to visit the launderette two streets away, to do each other's weekly load. Manoeuvring the metal twin pram was an unenviable task. I was weak and breathless, with a precarious load of washing and three restless children. Then the pram was stolen. "What am I going to do?" I complained to Sylvia.

As usual, Sylvia had a solution. She found a pushchair that I could use temporarily. But as I was wheeling it towards the market one day, there was an angry outburst.

"You black thief! You stole my pushchair."

I protested: "It is not stolen; I am only borrowing it."

One idea of Sylvia's proved extremely fruitful.

"Coral," said Sylvia, "have you done the football pools before?"

"No, of course not. I have not got any money."

"Have you any spare at all?" she persisted.

"Just one shilling and nine pence," I replied.

Sylvia was undaunted. "That's the price of the cheapest coupon. You could do that one."

With her guidance I filled in a random set of numbers on the form and sent it to Vernon's Pools that day. I was awaiting notification of Matthew's discharge from St Helen's when I opened the letter the following week. I briefly scanned the words. Disappointed because it was not the expected confirmation from the convalescent home, I threw it down on the floor, narrowly missing the fire.

Some moments later the reality of what I had just read began to register. Retrieving the discarded letter, I read it again with avid interest. I had selected the winning scores of the football matches played across the national league that weekend. My meagre 1s 9d (about 9p) had provided a handsome £214. 17s 6d (about £214. 87) return. Grasping the letter, I hurried downstairs to tell Sylvia the news.

When the money arrived, I gave Sylvia £10 and, since Royston learnt about my winnings from Sarah, I was forced to give him £30 for a car. I used the remainder for weekly down payments of five or ten shillings (25 or 50p) for a bed, dining suite, cooker, fridge and washing machine when I got my own home from the council.

My own home came sooner than expected, but not without some swift thinking. My name would be at the top of the housing list if the Bethnal Green property was kept clean and tidy. Domestic chores had been a way of life since I was four. I had grown up in a strict environment. Keeping house was not a problem – until I was whisked away to the Lower Clapton Hospital, near Dalston, for an operation.

It was four days before Christmas. The children would be returned from their foster homes by the authorities following my imminent discharge from hospital. Weak and crippled with pain, I had been unable to clean my home before my admission. I needed to ensure it was in order when the social services department arrived with the children, in order to maintain an unblemished domestic record and keep abreast of the housing queue.

Waiting until matron had completed her ward round, I moved hastily down the corridor towards the nurses' locker room. Sliding inside the door, I turned on the light and reached for the cupboard door. The uniforms were hanging neatly across the rail. Choosing one of the smallest, I quickly dressed, hid my nightdress and left. I caught the bus home and carried out a rapid spring clean before gathering up some clothes and returning to Dalston.

When I sneaked back to bed there was commotion.

A grim-faced matron announced: "The police have been out looking for you. Where have you been?"

"I went home to get some clothes. I did not have anyone to get them."

"You should have asked," insisted matron.

"There was no-one to ask."

I started to cry. The interrogation ended, and matron changed her tone. "Never mind. Come and have a bath and some cocoa before you go to bed."

The children were taken to foster homes in Essex and Suffolk just weeks later, before twins Marvin and Leo were born in January at the Maternity Hospital near Dalston. There were no visitors to break the constant routine of feeds and nappies from dawn until dusk. I was lonely and tearful, craving sleep and company.

I wanted an end to this enlarging family.

"Your husband will have to sign the consent form if you are sterilised," said the consultant. There were constant telephone calls and inquiries to find Royston. Finally he surfaced. He shot through the swing doors of the hospital at Lower Clapton. There was a resolute gaze as he approached my bed.

"You want to be sterilised? Well, you will have to pay me £20 if you want me to sign the form," he announced.

I did not argue. I withdrew my savings, every last sixpence and shilling that I had put away over the weeks and months. Within ten days of giving birth, the operation was complete, and I returned home.

"Have you got my two sisters?" asked Sarah, hurrying towards the front door when I arrived.

"You have not got sisters; you have two brothers," I said, motioning towards them.

"Take them back. Take them back. I do not want them," yelled Sarah.

Tears soaked her pillow that night. The following morning she picked up Leo and tried to push him through the window. But she soon got over her initial reaction. She warmed to the twins with growing delight, cradling them in her arms and rocking them in their beds. She catered for their whims and controlled their tantrums. She nursed them through illness and cheered them along the path to childhood. She was an indispensable pair of hands.

Six months later we moved to Wapping. In the 1800s it had become a thriving port. Houses were squeezed between high dock walls and warehouses, and it took the brunt of enemy bombing during the second world war. Wapping's enterprising days were coming to an end with the advent of container ships in the 1960s. Many of the warehouses were bulldozed, and the Thames was now quiet. Wapping was wasting and asleep when we arrived. Its commercial vitality had slipped away like the passing of an old season.

Nevertheless the spacious four-bedroom flat with bathroom and toilet at Vancouver House was made palatial and comfortable with the hire purchase payments from my pools win.

Simple, cheap meals were cooked in the fitted kitchen, and there was harmony as friends, family and neighbours gathered around the huge communal dining table. Wapping was a close-knit community, woven together regardless of race, creed or colour. There was a simple honesty nourished by the milk of human kindness.

But those initial carefree days were plunged into darkness when Royston returned. He bellowed and raged, again making endless demands and terrifying threats. There was just £7 a week for rent, bills, food and clothes. It was a meagre sum compared with Royston's lavish spending. He was a dapper dresser who regularly visited the best places in town.

"If you want more money, you need to find work," said Royston.

His personal vendetta against Lee worsened. It was a cold winter's day as Lee warmed himself by the fire in his dressing gown and pyjamas. But Lee was too close. Suddenly there was a mighty uproar, as the little boy's clothes ignited. Royston and I rushed into the room as Lee screamed in terror.

"I told you not to sit in front of the fire," shouted Royston, beating him across the head while he was ablaze.

Lee was rushed to hospital. He was traumatised and in agony. His skin was badly burnt. He was given a high dose of morphine, but nothing could stop Lee smashing his cot as he rocked back and forth. It was so painful to watch. During his lengthy hospital stay he had to remain sedated: he was permanently scarred and left with psychological damage.

Royston was also obstructive, refusing to make the monthly, compulsory signatures for the hire purchase payments; so the furniture and electrical appliances were about to be returned.

Phyllis had previously pressed me to contact her if I ever needed help. Desperate, I telephoned. Her voice was kind and reassuring. "Do not worry. Send the payment book to me. I will make the payments, and you can repay me when you can."

Two months later, Phyllis sent the book back to me. She had paid off everything. Her generosity came after a stay in hospital, where she was looked after by a team of kind nurses from the West Indies. The hospital authorities did not permit her to buy them a gift to show her appreciation. Since the nurses reminded her of me, she allowed me to benefit instead, by settling the hire purchase agreements.

Chapter 7 **A teacher's footsteps**

Twenty years from now you will be more disappointed by the things that you did not do than by the ones you did do. So throw off the bowlines. Sail away from the safe harbour. Catch the trade winds in your sails. Explore. Dream. Discover.
Mark Twain [6]

"Mum, why don't you come to my school and teach? You taught in Antigua," said Sarah one evening. She had put her school bag on the table and was searching through her pencil box.

Sighing, I turned towards her. "I cannot come to school and teach like that. You need qualifications, and there are interviews to pass."

Sarah was insistent. She returned with fresh ammunition. "Mum, please come to school and see the headmaster, because everyday we have a different teacher and I cannot understand what they are saying."

It was midsummer. The sunlight danced across the soot-brick warehouses in the high street as I made my way to St Peter's Primary School. Having arranged an appointment to see Mr Williams, the headmaster, I was shown into his office. Sitting on the edge of a chair, I took a deep breath when he inquired about my visit.

"Mr Williams, it is like this. I have taught in the West Indies for a number of years after obtaining my senior Cambridge qualification, and I would be happy to teach at your school."

I spoke at length, outlining my former teaching experience. I had purposely kept abreast of my own children's education and been responsive to the pleas of help for outings and support. I recounted this and more.

Mr Williams nodded. "Well, Mrs Martin, I am impressed. Very impressed. But there are some formalities to consider before you could teach here. First I need to contact the education department at County Hall."

He reached a large hand across the desk and picked up the telephone receiver. Within moments he was initiating a conversation that would mark a turning point in my career.

There was a shortage of primary school teachers in England at this time. Government campaigns were launched in a bid to send new recruits into the classrooms to feed demand, since pupils across the London boroughs and provinces were frequently affected by the shortages.

With this in mind, I approached County Hall in Lambeth – the local government headquarters for London – with optimism. The impressive building stretched along the River Thames just north of Westminster Bridge. I dashed up the wide open steps, through the swing doors and along the sacred corridors in search of the education department. The sign was posted in large, bold letters on the door. I knocked before entering.

"Sit down, please," said the craggy-faced professor who was in charge of the panel of eminent educationalists.

Peering down his spectacles, he waited for me to settle as I discreetly brushed away the creases in my secondhand two-piece suit and gazed at a sea of sombre faces. Eventually he broke the silence. His voice was slow and deliberate.

"We do not usually take people who are not trained in this country, but the headmaster at St Peter's Primary School would like you to teach at his school."

The interview progressed. I talked liberally, answering the questions with detailed enthusiasm. Finally, they reached a unanimous decision. On the completion of satisfactory references and a medical, the job was mine.

A teacher's job in England would bring radical empowerment, but the successive chapters that turned a novice into an experienced teacher came with sacrifice, hardship and prejudice. What followed was long days, and even longer nights, for as long as I could remember.

It began on September 5, 1964. It was six in the morning as I wheeled the twins and Matthew across the river towards the nursery and made a speedy return to prepare the remaining four children for school. The first day was a tough introduction to East End culture – a distinct contrast to the class of 70 placid pupils in Antigua. Besides stretching my sanity and ability, it made my hands red and blotchy, because I was allergic to the chalk. It was a quick arrow prayer that saw the allergy disappear by the next morning.

Vast reserves of energy and experience were needed to govern the class of 35 pupils. Many of the ten- and eleven-year-olds were rowdy, rude and indifferent to learning. They bucked authority, broke the rules and disrupted my teaching.

Bringing order in an East London classroom brought about a necessary transition for me. The following year I made a vow to enforce strong discipline to control the unruly, boisterous youngsters, and by then I was unafraid of the opposition and unpopularity it might bring. I became adept at dealing with the sometimes hostile reactions.

They came first from Lionel. Small, mean, and with a nasty temper, he showed a dislike for me and my lessons. He launched a full-scale verbal attack one day in the classroom, calling me names and swearing at the top of his voice. After receiving a severe reprimand, he turned on me and kicked my shins, making them bleed where I had varicose veins. I was quick to respond and smacked him on the legs.

Mr Williams' normal smiling face turned grave and anxious when I told him. "You should not do that. You could lose your job," he warned.

The next day Lionel returned to the classroom with a triumphant smile. His dad, a huge, angry man in his mid-thirties, was with him, swearing and cussing when he saw me.

"What did you do to my son?" he bellowed.

Quietly, but insistently, I told him about Lionel's behaviour.

The man's eyes narrowed, as he faced his son. "Did you do that?"

Lionel stared at the ground. "Yes," he whispered.

His father walloped him in full view of onlookers. "Never, ever kick this lady again, or call her names," he bawled. "Never, do you hear? Never."

The black community was still a small minority, so my presence continued to spark disquiet, suspicion and abuse. When I walked the children to nearby St Patrick's School for lunch every day, there were derogatory, angry comments from parents.

"Take your black hand off my child," they screamed.

The colour of my skin aroused growing intrigue from pupils. When I fell over in the playground and cut my knee, there was an outcry.

"Look," shouted one boy. "Miss has got red blood."

I smiled. "I don't know what you expected. Did you really think I would have black blood?"

Domestic life, child-rearing and teaching. The unending schedule merged every facet of my existence. It also marked my independence, since my new monthly salary of £70 meant that I still had more than twice the money in my purse than I had with Royston's former handouts.

My growing finances enabled me to help Sylvia too. She would visit me regularly after I moved to Wapping. One particular week she was distraught. She and her five children were due to be evicted because her husband had spent the rent money on gambling. I was more than able to pay the necessary rent arrears, without asking for it to be repaid.

Wapping was a short stroll from the Tower of London and the city. It was surrounded by high-rise flats and glass office towers. Bowler-hatted gentry governed the wheels of commerce, while enterprising foreigners worked in the sweat shops of home-grown industry. Office workers promenaded down Cheapside and tourists mingled with Beefeaters. It was rich and diverse; hurried and relaxed.

During weekends and holidays the children and I joined the string of tourists, tracing the back streets of ancient London past the Prospect of Whitby public house – once the haunt of smugglers and villains, and more recently a riverside respite for film stars and the more notorious members of society. We caught the familiar red double-decker buses to St Paul's Cathedral, Westminster Abbey, Pall Mall and Trafalgar Square. We visited art galleries, museums, exhibitions and crazy cartoon shows. We lazed in the sun at Hyde Park with bread and jam and a bottle of fizzy Tizer, and fed the slot machines at the West End amusement arcades with our meagre pennies. Crossing the river to Greenwich, with its narrow maritime streets and flower-decked lawns, we scrambled uphill to the Observatory and the views across London before lying horizontal and rolling down again to the shrieks of children's laughter. We travelled, discovered and broadened our minds. It was an on-going leisure itinerary that continued during the long drawn out school holidays and my varied teaching posts in the capital.

There was an uneasy expression on Mr Williams' face when he announced a necessary change in my teaching routine a few years after I began. He moved to the left and right, shifting his tall frame uncomfortably behind his desk as he spoke.

"I am afraid I will have to cut back on my staff, Mrs Martin. It means I will only be able to give you three days' work a week."

There was a pause. "However," he continued with some optimism, "I know a headmistress who may employ you for the remaining two days if you are interested."

Mrs Charles ushered me into her office at Rutland Primary School and poured out tea for two. She was immaculately turned out and well-bred. Her darting green eyes were full of expression. She had pearly pink lipstick and a set of immaculate white, smiling teeth. Her sugar pink suit emphasised her manicured nails. Her auburn coiffured hair was offset against a full porcelain make-up. We talked amicably. The conversation was sociable, in fact almost trivial, until the tack changed.

"Now," said Mrs Charles, holding the front of her desk and rising to her feet. "I am just going to get someone that you know."

She breezed out of the door, returning minutes later with a pretty blonde-haired child of ten, who I recognised instantly.

"Mrs Martin!" cried Maria, her eyes nearly popping out of her head. "Mrs Martin, how nice to see you."

Before another word was spoken, Mrs Charles intervened. "You know this lady, don't you?" she encouraged.

"Yes, this is the lady I told you about," said Maria.

Mrs Charles' eyes were kind and unwavering as she fixed her gaze at me. Then, without hesitating, she reached her hand towards mine and shook it firmly.

"I look forward to getting to know you better, Mrs Martin, when you start here in a few months. Because," she said with emphasis, "anyone who is kind to Maria is welcome to teach at my school."

I was astounded. There was no interview, no formal form-filling, just an offer of employment that came on the simple premise of befriending sweet, round-faced Maria – my former pupil. Maria, who had lost her mother and was brought up by her father and who, on many occasions, joined our family for tea after school. She would sit at the dining table, like all my other children, grasping a mug of hot chocolate and eating bread and butter. Sometimes, while shopping at the market, I would buy her a secondhand dress or coat for the winter. When her father moved, Maria had changed schools and we lost touch.

At the Whitechapel school Mrs Charles had a deep and beneficial influence on all the children, evoking understanding and achievement. All who sat under the educational influence of Mrs Charles thrived – teacher and child alike. She was a rare jewel in the hallowed halls of education, who also took me under her maternal wing as my estranged marriage became more challenging and made my hair fall out.

There was no pretence with the headmistress, but a gutsy honesty that I grew to recognise and appreciate.

"Where did you buy that?" she asked in open disbelief and horror when I walked into the school reception hall wearing a new, black wig to cover the alopecia.

"Oh somewhere in Whitechapel market," I retorted.

There was a quizzical look on her face as she pressed her lips together. "Mmmm. To be frank, that does not look good at all. I will take you to my hairdressers in the West End and get you a nice one."

"Oh no. I cannot possibly let you do that."

Finances were tight, but I was also proud. However, reflecting on her comments, I replaced the wig with a new one from the market. This time it was stylish and sophisticated but with an exorbitant price tag. It made its debut to the rapt applause of the headmistress.

"Oh I do like that one much better. How much did you pay for it?" she inquired.

"Ten pounds."

"Well, it is money well spent."

There was a knock at my classroom door later that morning. She sent a child with a letter that enclosed a crisp ten pound note and a short, scribbled sentence.

"You look so nice in that wig, so here is some money to pay for it."

Her generosity continued with fruit from her garden and invitations to her office for a glass of sherry. Those initial teaching days were happy and fulfilling. They placed hope and privilege at the forefront of my life despite the dark traumas at home. They also provided new building blocks of experience. I grew intuitive to each child's needs – understanding, first-hand, the challenges of abuse, prejudice and poverty. It gave me a tender soft heart for those bent and disfigured by similar trials. I was patient, poring over pupils' remedial lessons. I was inventive, drawing from my native culture to bring interest. I grew observant, seeing each pupil's hidden strengths and weaknesses. I sought to address them all, conceiving plans to draw out potential and thwart the difficulties that blighted progress. I believe such personal virtues were awakened and nurtured by the loving hand from heaven because of my own pain and suffering.

It was this shared empathy that broke the formidable barrier between race, colour and culture in the classroom. For although I was black – blacker than most children had seen before – I was loved and accepted by many, and by none more than Linda. One bleak, wintry afternoon, as I dusted the chalk dust from my hands, I saw Linda lingering behind after the end of lessons for the day. When every pupil had left the classroom, she slowly and tentatively approached me at the front of the class.

"Miss," she said hesitantly. "I was wondering." She paused for a minute, before continuing. "Are you black or white?"

Baffled, I turned my full attention towards the little girl, whose eyes were huge and unblinking. "Oh Linda, look at me. I am black."

Her eyes started watering. "Oh please say you are not black."

"Why?" I enquired.

Her words came out in fast succession. "Because my next-door neighbour is black. He is really horrible. He broke into our house and our gas meter and stole our money. But you are not like that, so please," she implored, "say you are not black."

I sighed. Slowly and quietly I responded. "Linda, I cannot say that I am not black."

Eventually, there was resignation. "Well, I don't care whether you are black or white, I like you just the way you are."

When a new education era meant I had to leave, there were presents from staff and children, including a smart leather briefcase. It was also the day that I opened my heart to a tiny black-and-white cat.

"I have not got any money to buy you a present, Miss, but I still have something for you." Linda was clutching a meowing kitten in her small hands. She transferred the vulnerable fur bundle to my keeping; I was speechless and terrified. An hour long journey to my new home near Plumstead Common in south-east London stretched ahead. A journey that would now be shared with my feline companion.

I caught the train from Whitechapel to New Cross and a bus to Plumstead High Street, before asking a nearby shop owner for a cardboard box for the remaining walk home with my new pet. But somehow the kitten escaped my clutches and scampered around the shop premises before I could retrieve him. I was fraught and bewildered by the time he was safe and sound at home.

Didger was an instant success, especially with Lee. He talked to him more than anyone else, taking him to bed, wrapped in a blanket, until he grew bigger and fought for freedom. Didger made himself at home. He tapped on the window with his paw when he wanted to come in and crept onto the draining board to drink from the kitchen tap. He was a welcome addition to the family, despite my initial misgivings.

Chapter 8 **A new learning curve**

Take the first step in faith. You don't have to see the whole staircase, just take the first step. Martin Luther King [7]

Disappointingly, after all I had achieved, new teaching regulations in the 1970s meant I was prevented from continuing to teach in England without formal training. I could not waste my experience, which had made me thirsty for more, so I applied for a place at teacher training college. At Avery Hill Teacher Training College I would be groomed as a recognised, qualified teacher in England.

I wrote at length, enlarging on my own life story, for part of the entrance examination, detailing the harrowing accounts and the obstacles that had seemed impossible to overcome. The learned professor read it with interest.

"This story proves you have a powerful imagination," he said.

"No," I gently corrected him. "This is all true."

He proceeded to look at the other two written papers I had completed. There was a long, nail-biting silence. He squinted at length at the dense lines of writing, as he turned the pages intermittently. Finally, he placed them neatly and squarely on the desk in front of him. He strummed his fingertips rhythmically across their surface, deep in thought.

After a polite cough, as if to summon my attention, he began: "Interesting. Very interesting. You appear to have answered all the easy questions incorrectly, but the hard questions, which determine your IQ, are all correct."

A quizzical look was etched on his brow. "I wonder why this is?" he muttered, as though addressing the question to himself. (It was actually because I had been so nervous that I misread the questions.) "Well, no matter. You obviously have ability, so please go back and re-sit the first paper that was incorrect, only this time complete it in half the time."

There was a resounding note of triumph when he read my second attempt. "Excellent. Excellent. You have tremendous potential."

I received a grant to attend the three-year course at the Mile End mature student annexe of the college in East London. This intensive study began when I was 36, more than a decade after I first entered the classroom as a teacher in Antigua.

I would learn, increasingly, how to juggle a noisy, demanding household with long hours of study and a grant that was barely enough to cover our living expenses, since Royston refused to make any financial contribution. At times there was little in the larder and meals were minimal, although the children did have school dinners. Hasty, arrow prayers were sent heavenward, and provision came. Returning home, I found unexpected sacks of potatoes on the doorstep, or anonymous letters enclosing money.

Organisation was the key to masterminding a busy schedule, so I devised a chore rota for my children. Initially, there were protests and sibling rivalry, but they soon buckled down to ease the load, with Lee becoming an expert ironer, which earned him two shillings a week. I planned advance menus, and at the end of the week, when the money was gone, the children were encouraged to use what was left from the preceding shop. Some made weird but tasty concoctions, while the lazier ones produced a boiled egg or bowl of cereal.

I would rather go without than see them hungry. When I could no longer afford New Zealand butter, I bought margarine and wrapped it in the old butter wrapper, but the children always knew the difference. Despite bread on the table and drinking chocolate at night, Matthew would overplay the situation to his friends.

"We cannot afford milk for our cereal, so we have water, and we are used to eating the cornflake crumbs," he wailed.

Matthew was told to count his blessings, and not to lie.

After the children had left for school I was soon a passenger in my fellow student's car, joining the streams of slow-moving traffic at the Elephant and Castle roundabout before heading over the River Thames to the Mile End Road.

The studies were exacting and exhausting. They stretched my intellect for new understanding that required endless library trips to learn about Education Acts and the structure of English primary schools. I grappled with research and class theory as well as practical teaching sessions at three London schools. I chose Divinity as my main subject. "God, I am doing your subject, so help me," I prayed after my first essay about the biblical character, Daniel. I received a D.

When the children were in bed after tea, baths, stories and prayers, I set the table with seven bowls and mugs for breakfast the following morning. I worked tirelessly, hunched over the dining table, surrounded by notes and text books and drinking coffee as the children slept. The days and evenings merged into one. The church clock across the street struck its lonely vigil long past midnight, and sunrise broke across the chimney skyline before I crept into bed.

During my first teaching practice at Eveline Lowe Primary School, I was assigned to Miss Turner's class. She presided over her class like a clucking mother hen who did not take kindly to student teachers or their new ideologies. She was a young tyrant with blonde hair and short mini-skirts. Her eyes were piercing and wary like an eagle. Like every other student, I was relegated to 'first mate' on the tight, inflexible ship that she ran.

I was called on to clean out cupboards, wash the paint palettes and take the milk orders. There was no scope to teach until I tackled Miss Turner the week prior to my tutor assessment. With plenty of huffing and puffing, she eventually agreed to step down from behind the desk to give me free rein. The lessons flowed effortlessly during the college appraisal. Teaching was, as always, instinctive and stimulating, earning me a distinction from the college authorities and a note of praise from the school headmaster. He wore a wide, generous smile when he approached me at the end of that first trial period.

"Mrs Martin," he said shaking me vigorously by the hand. "I have to say you have stamina. You are the first student to have stayed for more than a week with Miss Turner. Well done!"

Despite the many challenges, I worked hard – but failed my first year of academic studies. Completely downcast, I decided to quit teaching before I was asked to leave. There was a huge lump in my throat as I peered through the frosted glass office door of the principal's office. I raised a feeble clenched fist and knocked on the door.

"Come in," sighed Miss Perry, running her fingers along the long line of books on the shelves adjacent to her desk. "Yes, Mrs Martin, what is it?"

Bracing myself, I gulped hard. "I am leaving, Miss Perry. I cannot pass exams and continue with this teaching diploma," I said in a hoarse voice.

Miss Perry was unperturbed. With her back still turned towards me, she dismissed the suggestion. "Don't be silly. Did I ask you to leave? If you did not do well in your teaching practice and your exam, you would have been called to the office and asked to leave, but I did not call you."

Her tone softened. Speaking slowly and deliberately, she turned, giving me her full attention. "Lots of people can pass exams, Mrs Martin, but not many have the teaching talent you have. It would be a waste to rob this borough, or wherever you choose to eventually teach, of the knowledge and ability that you have. You will, without doubt, be an excellent teacher. Now go back to your study because you are not leaving. Instead, I will provide you with extra tuition."

The extra support helped me gain a strong foothold on the ladder of progress. Teaching continued with a passion, as I repeatedly burnt the midnight oil.

My two remaining teaching assessments took me to the Lea Valley and to Newham. I kept a keen and calculated eye on every class member. There were those with sugar-sweet temperaments and others, like eight-year-old Charlie, who taxed my wit and nerve.

Charlie had few manners. He would regularly hurl a string of swear words across the classroom at me until he was challenged.

"Charlie Mackintosh, you are going to stay in and miss your playtime, and I want you to write down all the swear words you know."

There was a mystified silence. A surreal glaze came over his eyes as I elaborated. "Meanwhile, I will write down all the swear words I know, and if my list is longer than yours, you will stay in."

Charlie started to stutter. "Y…y…yours, Miss, wi…wi…will be longer than m…m…mine. I c…c…can't write them d… d… down."

"That's right, Charlie," I assured him.

He thought for a minute. "But I am going to get my dad, and he will come to the school and beat you."

I looked at Charlie. He wore a shabby, ill-fitting uniform, his hair was unruly, but he had a sincere expression on his face.

"Well, Charlie," I mused. "I shall call my dad. My dad is a carpenter. He has a saw, chisel, hammer and nails. He would chop your dad up like mincemeat."

Charlie's eyebrows shot towards his hairline: "Does he really have those?"

"Oh yes."

"Miss, you promise not to call your dad, and I will promise not to call mine."

We soon struck a deal, and Charlie quickly mended his ways.

I finished my final teaching practice. It was the winter of 1973, and my college course was coming to an end when I was taken into hospital for a hysterectomy. I was ridden with fear and anxiety. My weight had dropped from nine stone to just over seven because of complications. I was tired and worn out. Royston looked after the children, but he soon grew impatient. His daily unannounced visits sent my blood-pressure sky high. He circled the hospital bed. His heavy footsteps tapped out a furious pattern on the lino floor.

"When are you coming home?" he bawled. "I cannot look after these children any more. Either you come back or they will be put in a home."

When my hospital discharge finally came, there was no opportunity to convalesce at home. I tackled the daily chores and considered returning to college.

It was the beginning of new year. I sunk my hands deeper into my coat pockets as the snow flurries danced across a colourless sky. My pace increased as I walked towards the hospital to see the consultant gynaecologist who would check my post-operative progress. Dr Stebbings' office was bright and spacious, lit by a single fluorescent light. After thoroughly examining me, he returned to his seat.

He was candid. "If you want to go back to college in six weeks, it will be tough. You will need to lie on your back on the floor every day and imagine you are pedalling a bike to strengthen your tummy muscles."

Between swotting for my final exams and writing an 1800-word dissertation, I made a determined effort to comply with his orders. On February 14 I was given the all-clear from the hospital and returned to college.

By this time I had joined the local community relations association through my meeting with John Waters. John was tall, lean, with an easy-going confident manner, and he was both likeable and kind. He had an ability to stem the widening cultural gulf with tact and understanding. His brief, as a voluntary community relations officer, was to forge ties with the immigrant community. He was informed and helpful, networking with various organisations, spreading his influence like a sweet-smelling aroma.

He first appeared on my front doorstep with Lee. He was totally unfazed by new situations. Lee had caught his attention while wandering the streets of Plumstead. John had crossed over the road, smiling amiably.

"Any more black people round here?" he asked. Before long, Lee was pointing him towards home. "You just have to knock on Mum's door, and she will invite you in for a cup of coffee."

That first encounter with John Waters sparked an honourable, lasting friendship. Making himself at home, he chatted and laughed and drank endless cups of coffee. We sifted through our life stories and, with his suggestion, I began to attend the weekly community relationship meetings and events. He became like a favoured nephew, visiting regularly with various girlfriends. Eventually he introduced me to Hannelore from the nearby university, who was studying English and became his fiancée.

Some years later they invited me to their wedding in Dusseldorf – the commercial heartland of Hannelore's mother country. They paid for the trip, which saw me leave England for the first time since my arrival. After the cross-Channel ferry to Calais, the overnight train sped across Northern France and Holland before tracking south-west towards the steep, unbroken gorges of the Rhine and Hannelore's impressive family home – a spotless, mellow-timbered mansion with marble staircase and huge glazed windows, set within an orchard. I stayed for three days, practising my German learnt at evening classes, dining on apple strudel and mutton stew and sleeping in a massive bed. The wedding was a memorable celebration as my two dear friends tied the knot, vowing allegiance through the joys and sorrows of every tomorrow. It was particularly poignant, knowing my own marriage would always be a façade.

In the meantime, Royston's ferocious temper grew even worse as he ruled the household with a rod of iron. He stamped around like a mad man, breathing condemnation and terror. He was particularly infuriated by my studies. He tore up my essays and threw my books out of the house. The shock waves of such behaviour reverberated across the darkened recesses of my mind. I walked on eggshells – nervous and agitated. I was afraid to speak out, afraid to pursue justice. Eventually it was unbearable. With Hannelore and John's help I waited until Royston was out and left with the children.

The old Edwardian house was a derelict squat, but a way of escape. There were no locks on the doors, the windows were cracked, and the walls were emblazoned with graffiti. There was no electricity, heating or running water. The floorboards were rickety and unsafe. With seven children, I fled here in fear for my life.

John loaded his little bubble car with our belongings. After three trips we were installed in our new home down the hill from Plumstead Common, a short drive away. We slept on the floor, visited the launderette, and ate and showered at the university campus where Hannelore studied. While the children went to school as usual, I studied without interruption.

Two months later I gathered up my pens and books and left the squat after the children had gone to school. It was June – the morning of my final exams. The elm trees that lined the suburban streets were in leaf and the sun was shining. I took the road alongside the common towards the bus stop when a familiar burly figure came towards me. It was Royston. He swung from side to side as he loomed closer.

His voice was loud and menacing: "You had better get home," he bawled.

My stomach lurched. I turned in the opposite direction and started to run. My stride lengthened as I heard Royston's thundering steps behind me. My pace weakened. I was breathless and exhausted. His large hand wrenched at my coat collar, and I was dragged backwards. He pounded my face again and again with his large heavy fists. Bruised and bleeding, I fell on the pavement. I was alone and barely conscious. Someone must have called an ambulance.

The children were taken into care during my ten-day stay in hospital. I received stitches for the cuts across my face. I was unable to sit my final exams.

For years I had gone into hiding and left no forwarding addresses, but I was unsuccessful in halting Royston's quests to find me. He had stalked the streets of London and traced my path through friends, colleagues and acquaintances. Now I sought a divorce and changed my name. It seemed the last option available to rid myself from the repeated bouts of cruelty. I filed the papers with a solicitor, and the marriage was severed.

My personal tutor, Mr Holton, helped put me back on the path to education. The college vice-principal arranged an alternative way to qualify as a teacher, since I was unable to take my final written papers. It meant being in the "hot seat" as I came face-to-face with the notorious tough examiner, Professor Craven.

"If you get through with him, your place is assured," said Mr Holton.

The professor's questions were hard-hitting and clever, but the answers easily rolled off my tongue, thanks to months of study and revision. I spoke about the Education Acts and I enlarged on ideologies, trusted teaching methods, government guidelines and the benefits of parent participation. The lengthy combat was over. I later faced an eminent bishop to test my knowledge of divinity and succeeded against the odds in becoming a qualified primary school teacher. I had leaned increasingly on the everlasting arms of almighty God, who secured my future prosperity with plans that continued to be written and sealed on heaven's parchment by the master author himself.

I secured my first post at Earl Rise School in Plumstead. It was a short walk from my home, which I reclaimed with the children after Royston was forced to leave. I continued at the Church Mission, which I joined on moving to South East London and where I met Hazel, a nurturing influence, who often invited us for meals.

Hazel had walked through the fires of trial and adversity. She had her faith in Jesus tested in the deep waters of trouble. She pored over Bible verses and was strengthened and encouraged by the age-old stories of prophets and shepherds, of warring kings and feisty women of mission – women who saved nations and fought contenders on the battlefield of faith and victory.

She gave me a plaque that featured a simple verse of Scripture. It became a treasured possession – propped up on the mantelpiece at home. It conveyed God's truth and fostered faith as I read it daily.

"I alone know the plans I have for you – plans to bring you prosperity and not disaster, plans to bring about the future you hope for. (Jeremiah 29: 11)

The judicial system moved slowly, but eventually Royston was sent to prison for his vicious attack against me. The court case hit the newspaper headlines. The terrifying drama was related to an unsuspecting public. In an instant my anonymity and privacy were wrenched away as I was called on to give evidence at London's Old Bailey – the highest court in the land. Instead of fear and shame came a determination to tell the truth, knowing that this alone would set me free. The facts were confirmed by letters from hospital doctors, and the judge was outraged: "This man should not be in your life," he declared.

Royston was sentenced to three years in prison.

Chapter 9 **Angel encounter**

***Do not go where the path may lead; go instead where there is
no path and leave a trail. Ralph*** *Waldo Emerson* [8]

The day after the prison sentence heralded a new and decisive
chapter in my life. The wheels of change turned quickly at the
education office when I told them I wanted to leave London
–to turn a new page and forget the bad press, public headlines
and reminders of Royston's old stomping ground. I needed a
break from the vivid, repeated memories of my torment.

The answer was Thetford. The town was a growing overspill
from London, near the Suffolk border – rural and flat and
surrounded by acres of pine forest and close-knit villages. It
had seen rampant expansion. A mixture of traditional town
dwellers and a growing influx of 5000 Londoners, who were
thrust into a new kind of life from the 1960s. Housed in specially
built rental homes, they helped feed the growing employment
opportunities that came from relocated businesses. Here was
a town that rippled and was marbled with a growing economy
and expanding geography – a rich interlace of people, culture
and enterprise.

I took the fast train from the main London terminal at King's
Cross – through the metropolitan stations and city fumes.
The sky-high terrace blocks and sprawling factories gave way
to open pasture dotted with cows and sheep. On towards
Cambridge and Ely, careering alongside slender pine trees and
open pig fields to Brandon, and finally Thetford.

I was due to meet the headmaster at Queensway Middle
School – one of seven schools with vacancies in the town.
Mr Carter was a kind-hearted, gracious man who helped pave
my future path. He listened intently to my story, introduced me

to the staff and secured my teaching post at his school with Thetford''s education officer, Mr Douglas.

From him there was no formality; just a simple a question. "How do you like Queensway School?"

Unable to contain my enthusiasm, I replied: "I love it."

"Well?" he said, turning to the headmaster.

"I would love to have her here," he said.

Thetford became my home in the summer of 1974 – a place where I could forget the former things and embrace a new future. My four-bedroom spacious town house was typical of the neatly boxed properties that lined the housing estates beyond the old town perimeters. It had two toilets, bathroom, integral garage, kitchen overlooking the back garden and an upstairs sitting room.

From the outset I was forced to stand my ground with one neighbour, since we were the only black family living on the Abbey estate. Johnny was a little boy who was unaccustomed to the colour of my skin. He would call out from the garden: "Blackie, blackie."

I watched and waited as his chants continued. "Come here," I retorted. "What is your name?"

"Johnny, Miss."

"Would you like me to call you ginger because you have ginger hair?"

"No, Miss."

"Why call me Blackie, then? My name is Mrs Martin."

"Sorry, Mrs Martin."

The brief exchange led to an ongoing friendship. He became a familiar figure at the garden gate, asking for jobs to do. I obliged, and gave him slices of bread and jam to eat.

While my children enjoyed a holiday in the country I made our new house into a home. Friends from London gave me curtains, and I borrowed money for carpets and lights. As always, finances were tight, but they were stretched and strained to provide for our needs.

Such provision came through constant prayer. Sometimes it was unexpected and divinely imparted, never more so than just before the children were due to begin school. There was a financial shortfall, since my new employment did not coincide with leaving Plumstead. We may have been the only Caribbean family in the vicinity, but I wanted my children to face their new schooling with all the privileges of white children. This included a smart wardrobe, although there was no uniform requirement. I looked in my purse. It was almost empty. There was little hope of any more money. I was a stranger to Thetford, so there was no-one to help. In desperation, I went into the kitchen and prayed. It was a prayer of faith that sprang from the depths of my heart.

"Dear Lord, you look after the birds of the air. You feed the animals. You know every blade of grass and know how many sands there are on the seashore. Now I am your child and I know that you care for me and love me. I am asking you, dear Lord, to please, please send me some money to get some clothes for the children. Thank you. Thank you."

No sooner had I finished speaking than there was a knock at the door. Standing outside was a lady with white hair, wearing a floral summer dress. She handed me a brown envelope, saying: "This is an answer to prayer."

Amazed, I inquired who she was and where she was from.

She simply replied: "The Lord has asked me to give you this."

Despite offers of hospitality, she left as quickly as she appeared. I never saw her again. Inside the envelope were five crisp £5 notes, enough for all my children's needs. I believe she was an angel of mercy, sent by God.

I soon grew accustomed to Thetford's timbered houses and ancient monuments that straddled the river walks; the modern purpose-built architecture that sprawled beneath a vast Norfolk sky; and to Queensway Middle School – a one-storey building with wide glazed windows that sparkled and shone in the late summer sunlight.

It was a half-hour walk to the school from Chester Way, through the developing estate, alongside the river and on to Hilary Road. A domestic timetable began each evening, ensuring the whole family were ready for lessons at nine sharp every morning – at various schools. Prayers and supper, homework and baths, with the children laying the breakfast table for the following day – it was a wearying, daily procedure that became engrained like a good habit. Without such rapt attention to organisation, it would have been chaos.

I was the first black teacher in Thetford. I approached my first day with trepidation, writing each child's name on the back of their chair in preparation. I prayed all day, but I need not have worried. The children were receptive and well-mannered, unlike those in London. By the time my own children were ready for school, there was no time for me to have breakfast. Instead, I took a pack of biscuits for the mid-morning break, which I shared as the youngsters drank their milk.

"I do not mind you bringing biscuits, provided you have enough for everyone," I reminded them.

There were never any offerings except my own.

As usual, I went to great pains to encourage each child to speak up if they did not understand. The hard regime of my own schooldays, when pupils were thrashed for failing to grasp the lessons immediately, made me particularly sensitive to their fears and needs. Those difficult early years in Antigua gave me empathy and wisdom for many of the ensuing challenges.

Tommy had a reputation for stealing, which I ignored until I found it was true. My rubbers, pencils and bright marker pens were always kept in my desk drawer. One day, I told the class that the markers were gone. Tommy was quick to respond. With a wide, gleeful smile he held out my familiar markers: "Here, Miss, you must have mine."

I called him to my desk. "Come and sit on my chair, Tommy," I motioned. "As you can see, I have an assortment of pens and pencils. I want you to make sure no one goes to my desk and takes anything again."

Tommy was ten years old, but it was as if he suddenly turned 20 as he rose to the challenge and mended his ways – until one particular incident.

"Miss, I am in love with you and want to marry you," said the freckle-faced lad as he handed me a huge diamond ring. I was 40 years old – too old even to be his mother. Lost for words, I gazed at the glinting jewel that was mounted on a gold band.

"I cannot possibly have this, Tommy."

There was an awkward silence. Tommy looked embarrassed. He shuffled his feet from side to side and looked away from me. I had no alternative but to place the matter in Mr Carter's hands. He summoned Tommy to the office after informing his mother, who came to the school. But by the time she got there, Tommy had disappeared. He fled from school to avoid the investigation, only returning after his mother had left – with her prized ring.

Tommy appeared sheepishly at the classroom door.

"I did not want to get you into any trouble," I insisted.

There was an angry response: "You should not have grassed on me."

"Well you must never do anything like that again."

The little boy was repentant. "I won't." Instead he came bearing gifts – cakes wrapped in toilet paper – and knocked on my door for jobs to do.

Over the years my heart ached for many of the children I taught. They came from diverse backgrounds with different problems. Hurting, poor, underprivileged and disabled. Those bullied and vexed by their peers or over-indulged with material possessions, but still aching for love.

It was a few days before Mother's Day at Queensway Middle School. The first signs of spring had come after the long winter. The air was warm and fragrant with the early blossom. Primroses and willow trees, dappled and ochre-green in the watery sunlight, lined the banks of the River Thet. It was a day like any other in early March – until something unforgettable happened.

In the classroom the children made cards and gifts for their mothers. The creations were inspiring and lavish, with ribbon, lace and carefully printed text. I addressed the class before they left: "On Mother's Day I want you to tell your Mum how much you love her, and thank her for all the wonderful things she has done."

Immediately, there was pandemonium. Hands were raised as youngsters told stories of how they would make the day special, with breakfast in bed, flowers and presents. Before mid-afternoon the excited cheers and chatter were a distant echo down the corridor. They were gone, except for one child – Alan. He approached my desk, speaking slowly and purposefully.

"I have not got a mother, Miss."

A tide of sorrow swept over the little boy. "My mother died when I was six, but I have got a locket of her. Would you like to see it?"

I nodded.

"I shall buy some flowers and put them on her grave and tell her how much I love her."

Tears rolled down my cheeks. His little arm came round my waist as if to bring some comfort. "But I have a dad who looks after me and my brothers. Have you got a dad, Miss?"

"No."

"Poor Miss!"

Afterwards there was a growing understanding between us. "It is my birthday soon," announced Alan one day. "Would you make a cake?"

It was a simple creation with icing and sweets and Happy Birthday scrawled in big writing. The cake was shared with 25 pupils, with some remaining for the rest of his family. The next day Alan's face was forlorn.

"I never got to eat the cake at home," he explained. "Walking home, I was so happy, I was swinging the bag of cake back and forth, and it went flying. It landed on the pavement."

Those days were like heaven's bounty for me. There was joy and endless happiness as I immersed myself in teaching. The classroom was filled with laughter and learning, as Mr Carter tip-toed past, as if to keep a keen eye on my progress.

I would take a brief stroll in the school garden, among the poppies and apple trees, as the children continued to work. I recalled the words of my former college tutor. "To be a teacher you must be good, but to be a black teacher you must be very, very good." The words resounded in my ears until I asked Mr Carter to assess my class in my absence and give his verdict.

"There is nothing wrong with your teaching," he announced. "You are an excellent teacher."

I had started to learn to drive in London, where I also took car maintenance classes. The roads were busy and bewildering, and my children were demanding. It was hopeless. But a year after arriving in Thetford, I tried again.

"After five lessons, if you think I am no good let me know," I told Mr Hagar, the driving instructor, "because I have not got the money to waste."

He agreed, but later insisted I needed ten lessons. Progress was slow. I failed to grapple with the gear stick, my foot revved on the pedals when it should have hovered. I was flustered and unco-ordinated in the driver's seat, failing to win the confidence of Mr Hagar.

"School teachers are the worst to teach to drive," he muttered when I ended my lessons.

Unable to accept failure, because God can make all things possible, I opted for a car with automatic controls, and tuition from my friend Karen Wright twice a week. She was patient and encouraging, taking me on familiar highways and byways to negotiate narrow streets, amber lights and three-point turns.

Friends from London helped me buy my first car – a beige Mini, small and set close to the ground. "It would be ideal," they enthused.

I was doubtful. "I have not got the money."

"We will lend it to you, and you can pay us back when you can afford to."

A few weeks later the car was mine. That October I took my driving test, but failed when reversing around a corner. A second attempt the following month also brought failure. Undeterred, I enlisted another driving instructor with a dual-controlled vehicle for a few lessons – and a further test at nearby Bury St Edmunds.

The Suffolk market town was bustling with eager shoppers for the festive season. Fairy lights blinked outside old gnarled buildings, and decorations arched the main thoroughfares. The slate sky overhead would bring twilight by late afternoon. It was a typical December in a thriving community, but for me, it was like no other. Fear and trepidation left me quaking behind the steering wheel as I left the test centre. Tears spilled when I successfully reversed around the corner and turned right but indicated left. There was more emotion when the stern-faced examiner turned to me with the words: "I am pleased to tell you, you have passed."

My success was not a secret. Mr Carter was at the test centre, since his son was ready to take his test. Learning the reason for my tears, he immediately telephoned the school, and I returned to a celebration. There were flag-waving children at the gates, and the staff presented me with a cake. One pupil left for lunch, returning with a huge card inscribed: Well done. I knew you could do it.

With new confidence I ventured onto the motorway for the first time, with my "Learner" plates foolishly in place. I kept in the fast lane without exceeding 40mph, infuriating other road users, who constantly honked their horns. Returning to Thetford, I was cautioned by the police until they found that despite the Learner plates, I was qualified to drive alone. My licence provided new found freedom. Gone were tiresome school journeys and irksome shopping trips.

In the summer of 1976, England experienced an unprecedented heatwave. The long, hot, balmy days, with outside lessons, alfresco eating and riverside dips, were more akin to Antigua than Western Europe, but the season came and went like any other. The trees turned russet and gold in the fading autumn light, the nights drew in, and winter fast approached. The change in weather also marked another season in my life.

Carefree days turned dark and formidable with Royston's return, just before Christmas. He appeared at the door with a suitcase, having been given early parole after serving two-thirds of his sentence. His prison years had been traumatic. He threatened to kill himself by drinking paint and hanging himself – psychiatrists believed he was mentally disturbed after witnessing his mother's adultery as a child.

Seething with anger, he faced me across the doorway. "Why did you change your name?" he barked. I was too flabbergasted to reply. I shrank against the hall wall as he strode inside and Sarah ran upstairs in fear. "I don't want him back. I want him to leave," she cried hysterically.

Despite all I had done, my whereabouts had been disclosed. The brick wall of solidarity and silence among family and friends had cracked. Sarah's mounting grief had spilled over into her conversation with her best friend, Celia, and she unwittingly gave away our new identity and our new address. After leaving prison Royston visited Celia's mother in a bid to find us. Apparently distraught and repentant, he pleaded for my address so that we could be reconciled.

With his appearance came a cruel, audacious threat. It sent shivers down my spine. "I do not want the children called Porter any more. I want them called by their real name," he bellowed. "If you do not agree, I shall tell the school authorities you are a teacher with illegitimate children."

I was distraught. There were flashbacks of Antigua, when my teaching career was on the line. Fear trampled my judgment. My breathing became shallow. I began to panic.

"What am I going to do?" I cried.

"You have got to marry me again."

My second wedding was without formality or celebration. It was over in minutes – a short, stark service in a registry office, far away from friends and family. It mocked my sanity, tore at my nerves and immediately and incomprehensibly chained me, and my children, to a tyrant again. It was the worst decision of my life.

The house that heaved with the children's friends now sighed with emptiness. Those who lined up in the kitchen for banana fritters and crowded the living room floor, eating biscuits, no longer came. Those who often slept on the lounge floor – sometimes a dozen or more – no longer stepped over the threshold. My home was strangely silent, sinking under heavy oppression.

Royston was still a bully who dominated our lives. He lashed the boys with a piece of copper wire for not making the beds properly. When they played marbles, he hit them over the head. I cowered beneath his ugly demands, too afraid to retaliate. Although I was quick to be subservient, I often went to school bruised and with black eyes, but I never took time off work. He pressed me into service like a maid employed by her master. I was cook, cleaner, chauffeur and breadwinner.

One Sunday I cooked a massive dinner for the family, ensuring there was enough to reheat the following day when I returned to work. It suddenly provoked Royston to more anger.

"What have you cooked all this food for?" he ranted as he walked into the kitchen.

Turning towards him, I answered calmly: "Some of the food is for tomorrow, so I do not have to cook again."

There was mounting fury in Royston's eyes. He gathered up the meal and threw it into the garden. Incensed, I reached for the boiling saucepan of water on the stove and poured it over him before banging him across the head with the empty pan. While Kevin called an ambulance I ran away, afraid of what I had done. "Call the police and lock me up," I cried remorsefully to a friend.

Royston remained silent about the incident, and no-one called the police. I visited him during his ten-day hospital stay, as he was treated for burns.

"You know I am not an aggressive person, but look what you have made me do," I protested in despair.

A few months after his return, Royston accompanied me to London. On our return, he grew angry and impatient, glancing at his watch for the umpteenth time. "Pull over," he demanded.

Royston had no insurance and did not possess a driver's licence, but I was too terrified to argue. I signalled right and pulled into the lay-by ahead. He shifted into the driver's seat while I became a front-seat passenger. He rammed the car into gear, and it flew forward. Within 100 yards he had driven into the back of a Mercedes. Thinking quickly, I took the driver's seat to take the blame for the incident before the police arrived on the scene. I was treated for cuts and bruises in hospital, and my car was a write-off. Royston left the scene without driving convictions.

But there was a greater cost. Minis had become highly sought-after as collectors' pieces, and within the next week mine had been due to exchange hands for more than £700 profit.

Now it was almost worthless, and I was without a car until I could save for another.

Royston made a habit of chancing his luck behind the wheel. Eventually, the law caught up with him, and he was sent to prison for driving while disqualified. It meant even leaner financial years, since I was left to pay his debts.

"Dear Lord, just help me," I cried in fear and frustration.

At the weekend a gleaming saloon pulled up at the front door. It was an unexpected visit from Denise, who had driven down from Lincolnshire. Stepping out of the car, she was greeted by excited, cheering children.

"Auntie Denise!" they yelled.

My tall, elegant friend approached the entrance, jostled between the oldest and the youngest child. With her arms outstretched in customary enthusiasm, she wrapped her comforting arms around me like a long-lost mother. "I just had to come to see you," she announced.

Minutes later, with tears and stutters, I recounted my terrible story. Perturbed but undaunted, she flung open the kitchen cupboards, made a quick inventory and took Sarah for a massive shopping trip, returning with grocery provisions. That weekend we cooked, ate and laughed until our sides hurt.

Denise was always a much-needed tonic. There were no limits to her kindness. She provided holidays for us in her Tudor manor house with its smallholding of sheep and goats, on the coast near Mablethorpe. It included a guest bedroom with an en-suite – just as she had promised decades ago, when we first met in hospital.

When Royston returned from prison, the anguish became intense again. I went for long, solitary walks by the river, tears pouring down my cheeks. If I took the children to church, there were more threats and beatings. Freedom to practise my faith was curtailed again – I was stopped from attending church, and I could not read the Bible. If I disobeyed there was bitter resentment, hostility and angry reprisals.

But God's word was hidden in my heart as a child, when I lived with Agatha. I had pondered and studied the words of power, truth and life. They remained with me – recalling them with ease in any given situation. In the darkest of valleys I was reminded to trust in the Lord with all my heart and not to lean on my own understanding. In joy, sorrow or disappointment God's word promised to strengthen, guide and help me. Only weeks before, I had seen this mighty God remove the disfiguring wart-like growths on my knuckles. Despite being removed when I lived in London, they had returned with a vengeance. For years I was shunned by pupils, who shied away from the terrible calluses, refusing to take my hand. But when I raised my voice in prayer, they mysteriously disappeared overnight, along with the resulting stigma.

I continued to sing and pray and weep for an end to Royston's torment. Desperate, I took matters into my own hands, pouring oil over the kitchen floor, hoping he would slip and break his neck when he walked through the back door. Suddenly I thought better of it. If you set a trap for others, you will get caught in it yourself, I reasoned with sound biblical sense. Hastily I cleared up the mess.

The school broke up for the summer – the holidays stretched before me. I became a play leader, planning fun, learning and leisure at the annual Thetford summer scheme. Although it was hard work, it provided a bridge to the community and a welcome separation from Royston. Again, there was respite… until I was rushed to hospital.

Royston accused me of stealing his wallet. Although I protested my innocence, he was unrelenting. "I do not believe you," he ranted. "You are a liar."

Royston's bloodshot eyes bore into me. He picked up a bottle beside the bed and thrust it into my face. Dazed, I fell to the ground. He stamped on my stomach. Blood poured everywhere. Royston vanished, and the rest of the night was a haze. Someone called an ambulance. The casualty department believed I had been through a car windscreen, since my injuries were so grave. I was too afraid of Royston's reprisals to tell the truth. I received 14 stitches and was treated for abdominal bleeding. I still bear the scars and a permanent black eye, more than 30 years later.

Earlier my son had been put on probation for playing on haystacks on private property. His probation officer visited me in hospital when he learned of the attack, but I was unrecognisable. He walked up and down the ward alongside the rows of beds. I waved feebly, whispering: "I am here. I am here."

He neither saw nor heard.

I was groggy from the anaesthetic and sore from surgery. The days were long, and my crying was relentless. Fear and despair knocked at my heart. Feeling wretched, and on the brink of ruin, I wanted an end to my life – to walk far away into the silence of the night and lie down for ever. It was the lowest time of my life. It seemed that every shred of hope had been torn away.

On the morning of my discharge Ed, who was married to my student teacher friend Phyll Jacobs, breezed into the ward.

"What you doing here?" I asked in amazement.

A set of brilliant blue eyes flashed back. "I have come to take you back to our place," insisted Ed.

The couple had telephoned the hospital each day since my admission, anxious to know my progress and release day. Their Norwich home, 30 miles away, was palatial, with six bedrooms, a huge kitchen-breakfast room and a well-kept garden. I was treated as a VIP, basking in the luxury of this little oasis while regaining my strength. Fed and pampered, I was also driven to the doctor's surgery to have my stitches removed. Yet despite the couple's pleas to tell the police about Royston's brutality, I remained fearfully tight-lipped.

There could be no going back to the family home, since my children and I feared for my safety. The six of them implored me to leave, with Sarah promising to look after the boys. I hired a room opposite the school to continue as a teacher. It was

lonely and small, but safe. Once again, I was back in harness
as a teacher, but I missed my own children – their individual
characters and special ways. There was a dull ache in my
stomach that tightened with anxiety when I thought of them.

The months passed until Royston forced yet another change.
He stormed through the school gates and into Mr Carter's
office. Fixing him with a steely look, he squared up to him as
if an opponent in the boxing ring. His shouting echoed down
the corridor, as his fury heightened.

"Tell my wife to come back home today. I mean today, because
if she doesn't, I am going to come here personally and take her
back with me." Eyes blazing, he turned and marched out.

Mr Carter's encounter with Royston brought a quick response.
"You cannot stay here now," he warned. "I am going to
telephone the education office and get you out of this area. Go
home and pack some things to take with you."

With a hastily filled suitcase of clothes, I was taken by taxi to the
school house at Watton, 15 minutes from my new post at the
town's primary school. It was cold, bleak and extremely lonely,
except for the elderly neighbour who cooked me a meal every
evening on my return. I poured myself larger and still larger
glasses of whisky and ginger ale at night to still my mind and
ease the isolation. It seemed a way to induce sleep and silence
the mocking, terrorising voices in my mind.

Watton was rooted in agriculture and was used as an airbase
in the second world war. Its quaint high street was steeped in
tradition and the tradesmen of yesteryear. Timbered, rickety
buildings with low-hung doorways leaned tantalisingly
across the pavement. But behind the old facade Watton
was in the throes of a modern-day revolution, with property
developments and emerging technology and commerce. It
was here, away from Thetford's cross-cultural divide, that

I settled, taught and became acquainted with an altogether different mix of pupils as their first black teacher. From the outset I was accepted. They were secure and happy with constant encouragement and careful discipline.

Rebecca's father was a farmer who grew strawberries. I ordered two punnets in the height of the season for just 20p each after Rebecca picked them. But it caused friction.

"Fancy taking money for them when you could have given them to Miss," protested her classmate.

Within a few days his mother appeared at the classroom door, laden with luscious strawberries.

"My son is full of enthusiasm for your teaching," she said, handing them over. "Before he left for school this morning, he asked me to pick these so you did not have to pay for then."

Meanwhile, the problems at the family home continued. Sarah and I would speak on the phone regularly and meet at the local police station every Sunday, since it was a safe venue. I gave her money for the bills but also learnt that Royston was threatening to harm me if I returned. Convinced Sarah was withholding information as to my whereabouts, he evicted her, and she was forced to stay with friends.

The family problems worsened when the probation officer contacted me about Marvin, who was grieving at my absence and refused to eat. I agreed to meet my son with Royston and the probation officer to find a solution.

The atmosphere was heavily charged. The four of us sat across the wide open table. For the sake of Marvin there seemed no alternative but to return. The decision came with Royston's vow that he would not lay a finger on me. Marvin eyed him suspiciously. "If you ever hit my Mum again I will kill you," he said.

Chapter 10 **Prime position**

A gift opens the way for the giver and ushers him into the presence of the great.
Proverbs 18: 16 NIV

At Royston's insistence, it was time to stretch my wings and look for another job. I applied to become an A team teacher – a highly regarded position in the London borough of Haringey. It demanded nerves of steel and an unusual ability to teach nursery or primary school children across this diverse region. The appointment would last a day, week, month or year – and on occasion two years – at any establishment.

The interview was gruelling. "What makes you think you can leave a quiet place like Norfolk and teach here?" asked the interviewer.

I emphasised my work at schools in the East End of London, but the pressing questions continued. "It is different here and different in this job."

"I am very adaptable," I replied.

That answer secured my role. The A team promotion became my flexible friend, enlarging my enterprise, developing resolve and bolstering confidence. It would hurl me into some of the most challenging positions I had known – jobs that many experienced teachers had quit before time. It would also bring rich rewards – camaraderie among teachers, parents and pupils and some of the most notable affirmations of my career.

I rang Sylvia for a place to stay in London. "You know you can stay any time," she enthused. Sylvia provided a comfortable home, with cooked meals and clean pressed clothes, without charge. I lived with her during the week and travelled back to

Thetford at weekends to pay the bills and do the family shop. It was a satisfactory routine until Royston pushed for a family home near my work; it was secured with a simple telephone call and a house exchange in North London.

Stamford Hill was my toughest teaching assignment. The deputy head had replaced the retiring headmaster. Teachers had come and gone after a few days with bad nerves and soaring blood pressure. I stayed the course but sighed with relief when the term ended. But even this school had its rewards in later years, when I met a former pupil who had taxed my staying power.

Ralph played football in the classroom and put drawing pins on children's seats. His antics increased until I caned him on the backside. He left the classroom and ran sore and crying to the headmistress, who immediately came to see me. There was an earnest, expectant look in her eyes.

"I was told by Ralph that you caned him. Naturally I refuted such an idea, saying that you are kind and would never do a thing like that."

Without remorse I confessed, and she left the room in silence.

Ralph was tall and mature when I saw him many years later at a London carnival. He had a wife and a cluster of children around his ankles. He waved enthusiastically, arms high amid the music and joviality.

"Hello, Miss. You were a wicked (awesome) teacher."

He turned to his wife. "This teacher taught me discipline. If it was not for her I would be in prison now, because I had such a temper and was so naughty."

A continual succession of positions followed my term at Stamford Hill. St Ignatius – a Roman Catholic school – could not have been more different. The pupils embraced me like a long-lost aunt. I had never been to mass before, so they staged one for me in the playground, and I celebrated their confirmations at the Catholic Church, when the girls were dressed as little brides.

The headmaster at South Harringay School was a keen Tottenham Hotspur football supporter who encouraged his school to wear the familiar white and blue colours. When he moved I was asked to take on the deputy headship. The promotion included lunch duty, increased paperwork and running two school assemblies a week, plus teaching a class of ten-year-olds. I took the role for the experience – it meant just 35p a day more in my wage packet.

We moved from our council house swap to a run-down property at Pickett's Lock when I bought our first house. It was cheap at the price, and ownership was secured with just £100 deposit and a 99 per cent mortgage costing £214 a month. Pickett's Lock was wedged in a provincial suburb that cried out for regeneration. It was drab and grimy with a crude hotchpotch of architecture – a forgotten reject on the northern fringes of the capital. It was without heart or vitality since enterprise, entertainment and employment were few and far between. This, then, was my new environment, where my quite unremarkable home was ragged and sagging at the seams.

From the outset it was a financial drain. Royston instigated a major renovation programme. There was dust, debris and distress for six months. My hair fell out and my nerves were shredded. Peace went out of the window as walls were demolished, windows replaced and central heating was installed. Tradesmen came and went. They left a trail of chaos when, critical and dissatisfied, Royston sent them packing before the jobs were finished, and the hefty deposits to secure their labours were lost. I got wise. I negotiated a quick exit and a fast completion with tradesmen before Royston returned at night. Speechless, he was unable to contest the calibre of work and delay progress again.

Royston's wish list was unending. There were additional measurements and quotes for carpets, a lounge suite and modified accommodation. Slick salesmen appeared regularly at the door with catalogues, brochures and assessments.

"Who is paying for this?" they inquired.

"She is," responded Royston, pointing in my direction for the umpteenth time.

Royston's wants plunged me into debt – debt that could have been crippling and frightening but for God's grace providing me with the means to work hard to repay every penny.

With employment at South Harringay School came my most alarming experience as a teacher, during a school trip to Dover that summer. We explored the cliffs – the stalagmites and stalactites – swam in the public baths, ran up and down the castle steps and rode aboard the miniature train. Finally, we took the cross-Channel ferry to France. It was a trip to beat all others, as the children learnt amid an action-packed programme, until a sudden deathly quiet silenced the excitement.

One little girl's sun-blazed face grew pale. Her eyes were beginning to close, and her body became limp. Suzie was a diabetic. She was always sensible, injecting herself with the much-needed dose of insulin, but our agenda had overrun, and she was urgently in need of her medicine. Returning to the camp where we were staying, she rapidly deteriorated. I fumbled with the needle. My hand was shaky and unsure. Despite every attempt, I could not force myself to penetrate her skin with the injection. I placed the needle in Suzie's right hand, positioning it two inches above the elbow, as I had seen her do. I pleaded for God to intervene as the crisis worsened and Suzie began to lose consciousness. Suddenly, her eyes opened marginally, and she purposefully injected the life-saving dose, reviving within minutes. Fear evaporated, as I gasped thankful prayers.

Before every school journey there were questionnaires for parents to complete, highlighting potential problems and illnesses. Gary's form never informed us that he wet the bed. He shared a room for a week with four classmates, and every morning his sheets were soaking. To avoid embarrassment, I washed the bed linen before breakfast in my room and hung it out to dry before anyone saw. Two days after we arrived home from the trip, a taxi pulled up outside my home. Gary emerged, carrying a huge box of chocolates as a thank-you. Further gratitude came from his mother, who spotted me in the bank where she worked.

Before the end of term, I joined my Class Six at the secondary school they would attend in the approaching September. Jason, a former pupil from Stamford Hill, spotted me during the children's preliminary visit. He was taller and more mature than I remembered, but he breezed over with his usual engaging confidence.

"Hello, Miss," he smiled. "Do you remember when you bust my mouth? We were boxing, and you gave me a sharp right-hand jab."

The listening pupils from South Harringay were astounded. "Miss, you did not do that?"

Slowly and deliberately I explained the story, much to Jason's delight.

During a physical education lesson, I was teaching the youngsters – particularly the boys, who lacked co-ordination and nimble footwork – how to skip. It was a slow process. Finally I showed them how to do it.

"Where did you learn to skip like that?" they exclaimed, gaping at my fancy steps.

"When I was a girl, I was a tomboy, and I was taught to do all the things boys did – football, cricket, boxing, you name it."

"You did boxing?"

"Yes, that is where I learnt to skip."

"You cannot box too?" said Jason in amazement.

"Put your guard up," I told him, clenching my fists. "This is what you do!"

"That is when I bust his mouth," I told the South Harringay children.

Jason nodded in agreement. "Don't you try any nonsense with Miss; she is good," he warned.

Despite the difficulties, I was not beyond saying sorry. Once, unknowingly, I reprimanded Ben Brown severely for a crime he never committed, and he left the class without protesting.

"Ben," I said, realising my mistake the next day. "I am very sorry to have judged you wrongfully."

This public apology caused some consternation – even tears – in the classroom. I said: "I am not too big to say I am sorry if I do something wrong."

St Michael's Primary School, Muswell Hill, was in a salubrious North London suburb. Most of the parents were well-paid professionals – solicitors, architects, doctors. Here, protected by influence and affluence, their offspring were wrapped in luxury and indulged by nannies or au-pairs. But for some it was not sufficient. They grew sick and insecure as they craved attention from their successful, globe-trotting parents. At school they sat on my chair and, resting their head on the desk, they clutched a "comfort rag" that I always brought to class. Within an hour or so, they were ready to resume lessons.

Many of the pupils would continue their education at state schools across the borough when they left my class. But Ollie was earmarked for the private school on the other side of the road.

Like his privileged counterparts, it meant segregation from the others, including his best friend. Ollie and James were like long-lost brothers – wherever one went, the other followed. Their separation hindered their happiness and learning until I resolved to place them together again, which prompted a letter of gratitude from Ollie's mother, a head teacher.

Parents and teachers alike were hesitant when I arrived. But as the days turned into weeks and months they reviewed their stance.

"When you first came here, we were apprehensive," said the head. "We had never had a black teacher at the school, but now you have colleagues and parents eating out of your hand."

It was praise that came, in part, from breaking the traditional "straitjackets" that had thwarted pupils' creativity. I dispensed with the precision colouring and perfect lines instigated by the art teacher, rather than the pupils. Instead I gave the children free rein – the resultant lopsided symmetry had the simple, honest charm of developing talent. Despite the art teacher's objections, the results were emblazoned across the classroom wall – much to the delight of proud parents when they saw their children's work for the first time.

It gave me a faithful following of parents. Some regularly joined me in the classroom.

"We would like to come and watch you teach," they said.

They arrived as spectators but they soon made welcome contributions – mixing paint, listening to aspiring readers and fetching coffee. Numerous invitations to dinner and children's birthday parties followed; there was rarely a day when I needed school lunch. I ate in elegantly proportioned homes – Victorian and Edwardian splendour with period charm – wooden floors and massive hallways and spacious basements. Homes decked with antiques that glistened with crystal, silver and mahogany.

Wading through thick pile carpet, I was ushered into a different world in this cosmopolitan suburb with its spectacular views over London. A world that gyrated with actors, artists and media people – a commuting bolthole for upward-spiralling professionals amid trendy bars, restaurants, coffee shops and delicatessens.

Friendships with parents and teachers alike continued. They included Jan, a nursery school teacher who I befriended after giving her a lift home from the bus stop. We would share the ups and downs of family life together for the next 30 years or more.

My confidence increased with my new-found popularity. I was inspired to use variety and creativity to kick-start lessons. Talking about my days in Antigua caught the imagination of pupils, causing them to count their many blessings. The colourful West Indies transported them to an unknown country of beauty and cruelty, of wild terrain and the sweetest pineapples, where poverty and prosperity, slaves and masters wrote its history and destiny.

My culture also brought a new culinary dimension to my colleagues when I announced I would cook for them. Twenty teachers dined on spiced rice, chicken and peas – Caribbean style – the meal more than funded with an unexpected collection of £70. The dish was so popular it became a regular fund-raiser at the summer fete and Christmas bazaar.

That summer pupils gathered in the waking dawn for the long coach and ferry trip to Le Touquet in northern France. The expedition through the Dartford Tunnel to Dover led to a breath-stopping halt at Customs after we read in the press that black people were barred from entering France at this time. But our journey was uninterrupted. Together with Class Six and a handful of parents, I slipped easily past the authorities and was soon crossing the swell of the North Sea to Calais and beyond – past grey-stone towns and villages decked with flags and scarlet geranium window boxes. On past the massive graveyards that bore witness to the thousands of young men who lost their lives during two world wars. Across the rural hinterland of rivers and agriculture, with ramshackle smallholdings complete with geese and hens.

Le Touquet came into view an hour later. It was a complex mix of English charm and French sophistication – of chic boutiques, patisseries, pine forests and winding roads. A summer playground of yachting, sailing and horse-riding where sand and surf kept the fun going on that joyous hot July day. Where youngsters buried adults chin deep in sand and drenched them with water. Where ice cream cones and sun cream mingled with gateaux and chips. The day that began slowly at dawn sped towards twilight, and the hushed stillness of the small hours. Adults yawned, children slept, the coach lurched homewards in the hastening light and waking bird call.

It was past 4am. Rather than returning home, there was a long-standing appointment at the family home of one of my pupils, who lived nearby. I was shown to the guest suite at the Rovers' house. It was a welcome retreat, since school beckoned only a few hours later, even though the children would not attend after the exhausting trip.

I knew the contours and riches of the house well through successive visits – they fostered rest and relaxation. But in the shimmer of light that pierced the early morning shadows, there was unexpected luxury – clean pressed night clothes, silk sheets, a satin counterpane – and later breakfast in bed. This black girl from the ghettos had, for once, broken every barrier between class and colour.

Mrs Rover was genteel, kind and hospitable. She possessed an inordinate amount of grace and style. Her creative flair, which her son Stuart inherited as an artist, flowed over every crevice and corner of that high-ceilinged home. It was opulence and order at its finest – ornate drapes, muted walls, serene lighting and striking prints against huge tan hide sofas. Texture and pattern, contemporary and traditional. Dark and bleached woods meshed with palettes of azure, ochre and emerald. It was, without doubt, an inventive hand at its most creative.

My initial contract at St Michael's School was for a year, but Mrs Rover's petition with parents' signatures secured a successive year for "inspired teaching", which I was happy to undertake. St Michael's became a landmark in my developing career, and I left with tears of gratitude to God.

But my time here also heralded another of Royston's terrible schemes. It was blatant and premeditated. It was evil and desperate. It had me reeling in horror and disbelief.

It had been a fruitful teaching day. Soaking in the sheer exuberance of it – smiling at the children's charming stories – I left the empty classroom as usual by mid-afternoon. My pace was brisk – a habit formed in Antigua, when I always hurried to keep up with Kettty's demands. I crossed the playground and headed towards the car park and my blue Ford.

Clutching a haphazard pile of exercise books under my left arm, I wrestled with the car lock with my free hand. Easing the door open carefully, I tossed the books onto the back seat and settled in the driving seat.

The journey took me through salubrious Highgate and Hampstead, past grandiose Edwardian semis – high and imperious above heathland and parkland and beyond the clatter and clutter of cosmopolitan living – misshapen dwellings and eccentric shaded neighbourhoods. Through traffic-choked suburbia – a changing landscape – to the inner reaches of Tottenham and finally Pickett's Lock. Criss-crossing and weaving around the clustered back streets, I eventually edged into the left-hand kerb until I reached the familiar wrought iron gate at Number 41. Suddenly my heart was beating furiously. There was a loud pounding in my ears. Outside was a huge For Sale sign. The agent's name was plastered in red, with a telephone number.

I pulled up the handbrake and turned off the ignition. I sat in silence. Unknown minutes ticked past on the dashboard clock – minutes that had no shape or form. Minutes without reason or feeling. Slowly, and all too surely, whispered words chased across my mind. They grew louder. They grew fiercer. They implanted terror, confusion and anger.

It was some time later when I turned the key in the front door. Through the hallway I could see Royston's wide shoulders bent over the kitchen work surface. His gnarled, coffee face downturned and intent on buttering some toast.

I took a deep, determined breath, walking into the small galley kitchen.

"What is going on?" I demanded.

Royston was silent.

"What's going on?" I asked again.

Royston gradually eased himself upright and turned to look at me. "I am going back to Antigua, and I want my share of the house."

Aghast, I argued that he had not paid anything towards the mortgage, and sometimes I had made personal sacrifices to I keep abreast of the repayments.

By now I was out of debt after Royston's extravagant property refurbishments, but the tight grip of financial oppression was to come again. I was still a woman who lived in fear. Less than five foot tall – slightly built – with the mental and physical scars of this man's incessant abuse. Sometimes those scars were raw and ugly, like festering poison. I wanted to finally break the stranglehold of fear, but I was still tormented – thwarted and intimidated by this heavyweight giant who seemed without soul or feeling. With a mind that was both genius and devious, he had launched yet another "master stroke", knowing I was too weak and scared to fight.

My house was worth £22,000 – he wanted £11,000. It was money I did not have; my only assets were tied up in the property. With Jan's advice, I borrowed £5,000 and recouped all my national insurance premiums in the hope of sending Royston to Antigua for a lifetime. He left with suitcases laden with clothes and our few possessions, including the hi-fi system. His departure was short-lived. He returned empty-handed three months later – half the money spent on riotous living.

Chapter 11 **Island of change**

God is the only one who can make the valley of trouble a door of hope. Catherine Marshall [9]

The airport terminal at Heathrow was buzzing with activity at dawn, when I took my luggage to the check-in for the flight to Antigua. I slept little the night before, not daring to tell Royston about my travels in case he put a stop to them.

There was a mixture of excitement and apprehension for my first flight, and for my return to the Caribbean after 25 years. I settled myself for the long haul across the Atlantic. As we ascended rapidly after take-off, England's rural and industrial tapestry below grew distant and disappeared below the cloud line. Nine hours later the plane circled and tilted towards the ocean. There was Antigua – a glistening, emerald jewel in the sunlight.

Twenty minutes later I was on home ground. It was summer, and the temperatures were sizzling: it was as if I had been blasted by a hot oven.

"How long are you staying?" asked the passport official.

I gave him a courteous smile. "I beg your pardon. This is where I come from."

It would be a fleeting visit to a new and unfamiliar paradise, where the trappings of colonialism, dogma and prejudice had quickly been abandoned. Now Antigua was an independent state. It was raising its own flag, determining its affairs through its own people. In 1967 – seven years after my departure – it became a self-governing member of the British Commonwealth.

It was an island of change. Familiar haunts had been erased or enlarged, and there were new attractions seething with

crowds. To make way for the buoyant tourist trade, the harbour
at St John's had also been dredged, and so ocean-going liners
docked at the quayside. Passengers stepped onto dry land
without the need for a launch and were whisked away to plush,
modern hotels by taxi.

Antigua had sprinted into the modern age. There were new
supermarkets, petrol stations and an upturn in living standards
that came largely from American influence, with the advent
of big brick houses and modern appliances, including huge
refrigerators. Those who had trudged the gutter in poverty
were now becoming increasingly prosperous as opportunities
for higher education were unveiled. It was a new culture,
running with the wind of change. It was one that I would have
been party to if I had stayed to catch the cultural tide.

Unknowingly my struggles against poverty, prejudice and
disadvantage had helped in a small way to change the face of
Antigua's education system. As one islander commented: "You
made history in Antigua, enabling children from poor areas to
receive school scholarships. You were the first to be denied
one, and the first to be given one. As a country we have fought
injustice to make sure it never happens again."

Despite an awakening era of hope, enterprise and awareness
of our African heritage, some things and some people did not
change. There were still those rooted in tradition – too old and
too comfortable to alter their lifestyles. Townsend was one of
them. Stooped over a furnace, wearing leather gloves in the
baking hot day, he worked the forge and anvil from dusk to
dawn, just as he had done decades before. Silently, he plied his
trade for a meagre wage, with many of the same customers.

Trusted friends from the past were still around, and some of the
historical markers – the tumbledown shack, and my first home
when I married – continued to scar the landscape.

I visited these haunts and more during my two-week visit while staying with a friend and relative of Aunt Violet.

I sat on the beach, where I caught cockles when I was barely five, now watching the ebb and flow of the tide while eating mangoes with my nephew. Travelling by bus, I went to see Molly in the country. She was a qualified teacher, with a private school at her large, airy house. I slept in a huge bed draped with mosquito nets and armed with repellents. We recounted the past, caught up with the present, determined the future and visited the Mission Church.

It too had changed. The pews were packed, and the people were raising the roof with heartfelt praise. There was singing and prayers, tears and joy. I recognised some people; they used to be gamblers and drug dealers. Now they loved the Jesus who cut their habits and saved their souls. Like countless others in the church that day, their lives had shifted into divine gear. A powerful move of God was chasing away the demons to bring health, hope and help – and it was happening at the church I was barred from for marrying Royston!

Those who turned their back on me more than two decades ago were no longer there. Only three of the original families remained. They held out their hands in welcome as I spoke about my return visit to Antigua. On leaving, I promised to send money from my monthly wage to support Pastor Lee, a dynamic preacher.

I wanted to address the past and approached Mr Hart's large, sumptuous home, that was dazzling white in the sunlight. The dappled shadows of a coconut tree danced across the entrance porch as I rang the bell and waited for the maid to answer. Greeting me courteously at the door, she showed me into the living area. Mr Hart immediately put down his newspaper and stood up. His once youthful face was more lined; his dark hair was tinged with grey; but he was still a tall and imposing figure with a broad, engaging smile.

"Coralita, what a surprise. How lovely to see you."

He motioned me to sit down, and I sank into the sofa and accepted a cup of tea.

"Mr Hart," I said after the formalities were over, "I have brought you some money to repay the loan for my passage to England."

"No, Coralita, you do not have to give me anything. That was a gift, and I am glad that you have made it as a teacher."

Making my way onwards to the cathedral and the centre of St John's, I came face to face with an old friend. While we laughed and talked, a familiar figure approached. Aged about 35, she was smart, fashionable and glamorous. Her eyes darted with life and enthusiasm. "I knew it was you. I have never forgotten that laugh and that little mole on the side of your face," she said, drawing closer.

Looking more closely, I recognised the young woman as Karen Richards, one of my former pupils. From the outset there had been something special about Karen. At eleven years old she had grace, ability and a head for figures.

She had just emerged from a massive superstore. Taking a step back, I studied the gleaming, pristine building. Its colossal square-footage and wide glass windows were synonymous with an American-style retail outlet, and her name was emblazoned across the front – Karen's Superstore.

"Is this yours?" I exclaimed.

Karen nodded. Her astute, entrepreneurial spirit that was recognisable in the classroom decades before was now paying dividends. I could not contain my joy.

"I always believed you would make a good businesswoman, Karen, and now you have become one," I enthused. There were reminiscences and laughter in the long moments that followed. "Come in and look around, and choose anything you wish," she motioned.

Hesitantly I accepted. The store was a treasure trove of jewellery, cutlery, clothes and linens. Karen had priced the merchandise to sell for a swift profit. I chose a simple yellow T-shirt with a rainbow and the words Antigua – where land and sea make beauty. It is a prized possession even now.

Chapter 12 **Favour and furore**

My grace is sufficient for you, for my power is made perfect in weakness. *2 Corinthians 12: 9 NIV*

Mixed blessings followed. They began at Rhodes Avenue School, where I won quick rapport with teachers, children and parents.

"This is where your classroom will be," said the headmistress, motioning towards a spacious playing field. My new post was in a mobile classroom – that was yet to arrive.

Rhodes Avenue School, near Alexandra Palace in north London, held its head high in the prosperity and attainment league. Youngsters were given encouragement from an early age and inspired to follow their wealthy, privileged and successful parents' well-trodden path of responsibility. Such parents were an elite class of artists, seasoned professionals and entrepreneurs who were largely without pretension or social snobbery.

I inherited a class of ten-year-olds who were bent on learning, kindness and understanding – even when I was absent from the classroom. When I was late for school on one occasion I immediately informed the headmistress of my unavoidable delay, and together we dashed to the mobile classroom. Heads were bowed, and work was in progress.

Breaking the silence, the headmistress turned to the pupils. "Why did one of you not tell me your teacher had not arrived?"

"Oh we knew what to do," was the reply. I always chalked the assignment for the following day on the blackboard before departing in the afternoon.

Despite the hard graft, I was determined to make the lessons fun and, if possible, take learning beyond the confines of the classroom. During pets' week children bought cats, dogs, gerbils, hamsters – and even a snake – to school. As usual there were birthday parties for pupils and, not to be outdone, in June I staged my own, with dancing and games – and parents' gifts of cake, flowers and chocolates.

I also enlisted help from one parent who was a television newsreader. He outlined his job details in the classroom to help youngsters engage with local and international news during current affairs lessons.

Swimming, and visits to my home for tea with parents, went beyond the statutory curriculum. There was also a trip to the West Indies shop in Edmonton on a red London bus, to buy coconut buns and sugar cane to suck. The unique experience meant a first-time bus ride for the many accustomed to being driven everywhere by parents and nannies.

Teaching at St Paul's and All Hallows in Haringey brought new challenges. Two teachers made my life miserable. They berated me, scolded me and tried to undermine my confidence, despite my obvious success. I would grimace at their cruel remarks.

"Fancy putting sun cream on that child's back – if I was you, I would have slapped his back," said one teacher.

The education officer was quick to offer an alternative position. I resisted – it was nearing my last term – and I wanted to continue supporting the children.

I came to understand that the pressures of 20th century living were, in some ways, no different here from in the Caribbean. There was still abuse, injustice, suffering and terror. It was often hidden behind locked doors or masked by busyness and efficiency, but as a teacher I saw it mirrored in the children's behaviour – like black, indelible ink.

At such times being a teacher was never enough – I needed to be a counsellor. When I was up against it, fresh strength came with the rhythms of divine grace.

Terry's parents were ready to separate, and he was distraught. "My Mum and Dad are breaking up," he spluttered when the pressures were too much, when he was restless and tormented and his eyes were huge pools of water. I was at a loss to know what to do; I prayed, and finally I tackled his parents. They were forced to face the issues that were no longer just their own. With new resolution they were reunited as a couple, and Terry began to flourish again.

There was not always such a happy ending. Shane's father was an alcoholic whose addiction was like a rampant cancer, threatening family life. I knew Shane's mother. She was always there – always faithful – at teacher-parent consultations and school events. A frail, earnest woman, stooped under the pressures of bringing up her son in a home violated by drink.

One night she telephoned. She was desperate. Her husband had used the bread money to buy a bottle of rum – he had been drinking for the last two hours since arriving home. She was relating what was happening when she abruptly announced: "Hold on a minute. My husband is making a funny noise."

In a brief moment, the man was dead. He had choked on the liquor that had turned him from a gentleman to a tyrant.

It was a terrible night, but the weeks that followed were no better. The trauma that spun a mother and her young child around in loss and bewilderment threatened to engulf me. I fought the haunting reminders of Royston's hostility while comforting a grieving family that was plunged into ruin and loss.

It was at this time, during a writers' workshop for my class, that I was challenged again. Mary Hoffman was a prolific children's author who lived in Muswell Hill; to date she has written over 90 books. Her gift was refined in the white-hot heat of imagination, as creative prose and plots came to life off the page. She was also an experienced journalist and, as with many, she was a habitual story-taster – sifting wheat from chaff to find that all-time scoop. When I recounted some of my own experiences, she was jubilant: "Your story is better than The Colour Purple." Her wide, expressive eyes danced with joy. "You must write a book. It will be a best-seller! Start writing now," she implored.

The house was quiet as the children slept. My faltering efforts began. The first paragraph was incomplete, and the tears started to flow – they kept flowing. They fell in huge puddles on the lined paper and made the lines bleed. There were subsequent attempts, but all were abandoned after a few scant sentences. The pain was too great. The tears were too many.

The challenge to write my story would only come to fruition decades later, when the season was right – when I was a grandmother of 76, torment had finally ended and suffering had ceased like a worn-out disease. When written words were therapy and the story – for God's glory – was complete in his healing, restoring hands. Written to bring hope, strength and comfort to women, men and children – no matter how deep the agony.

In the meantime teaching continued. I stayed just a day at Bruce Grove – it was heart-wrenching to leave. At St Ann's I grew despondent; I was often called to do dinner duty while the teachers went to the pub. I left the post before time in a bid to curb the injustice.

The Broadwater Farm School near Tottenham was more challenging and distressing than any other. The community was ripped apart by poverty, racism and violence. The notorious estate was a grotesque blot on the landscape – a planning nightmare of large concrete blocks and tall towers built on stilts to avoid flooding; it dwarfed the neighbouring Victorian houses. A dire, soulless place, it originally housed up to 4,000 people but continued to expand. Poor maintenance meant water leaks, pest infestations and electrical faults. Its interconnecting walkways were isolated and dangerous, becoming hotspots for crime and robbery, with easy getaways. Within less than ten years the authorities believed there was one solution – to demolish the entire estate.

Most prospective tenants declined housing offers there, while existing ones applied to be re-housed elsewhere. It became one of the worst places to live in the UK – especially in the 1980s, when riots between racial factions and police made national, unprecedented headlines.

It was a neighbourhood in disarray. Life was futile. Hope was lost. Every afternoon of the six-month contract I left with a heavy, broken heart. I needed divine, daily refreshment to make it through those bleak, discouraging days. Youngsters were deprived and disturbed by the unending hostility and poverty that stalked the community. They were difficult to teach – tired, undernourished and confused. Five-to-seven-year-olds shared the same class, and the children who did not have breakfast drank their morning milk on arrival – which their parents also shared, such was the poverty.

My A team teaching ended at Noel Park School in Lordship Lane, Wood Green. The towering block, reminiscent of a Victorian workhouse, was situated in a multi-cultural community in north London. Twice a day, I climbed six flights of stairs to my classroom, despite painful arthritis in my knees.

The A team role spanned 11 years. It stretched my understanding and determination. I had taught in some of the worst and best places, but whatever the challenges and experiences, I knew I was richer for them.

Chapter 13 **Deliverance**

Faith makes all things possible - love makes all things easy.
Dwight L Moody [10]

The condemning echoes of the past and present grew more distant when I made a conscious decision to fight for my dignity – to fight for truth, despite Royston's jealous jibes and accusations.

Royston wanted to return to Antigua again and demanded another £10,000. This time I turned such demands to my own advantage as Royston slipped down the slope of self-destruction. My mind began to work positively instead of negatively. I determined to rid myself of Royston once and for all.

A new boldness came with my proposal. "First I want a divorce, which you must not contest, and I want you to renounce all claim to any property. You must agree not to follow me, leaving me to live in peace, and I shall give you £5,000."

There were no arguments. The agreement was drawn up as a legal document and signed by both of us.

The divorce came as I safeguarded my independence. Turning to my children, I was blunt: "If anyone lets your father back into the house, I will throw the whole lot of you out."

Shortly afterwards I was seething with anger. Royston's claims to poverty were never true, but now there was blatant evidence that he had more money than I ever realised. I was in the bedroom, which we shared, giving the room a thorough spring-clean, when I turned up the bed and removed the mattress – and discovered a secret stash of banknotes. It amounted to £800.

Royston returned from Thetford to London to stalk me.
Wherever I turned, he was there. He knew he did not love me
and he could not live with me, but it seemed he could not
be apart from me either. Waiting. Watching. He slunk in the
shadows – behind parked cars and in doorways across the
street. He sidled between the aisles in the supermarket and
leaned against the school gates. His haunting presence never
ceased. It was there night and day, invading my territory and
threatening my sanity, until a court injunction restrained him.

For some months there was peace, until I called a plumber to
mend the gas central heating system. His investigations caused
alarm.

"Call the police," he shouted. "Someone is trying to kill you."

He led me outside. The heating vents were blocked with paper.
The system had been purposely sabotaged so that carbon
monoxide fumes would fill the house.

Nothing could be proved, but Royston's desire to kill me resurfaced
later. He crept into the house through the upstairs bathroom
window, brandishing a knife, thinking I was alone. It was dark. I was
asleep, but Matthew's friend was staying overnight.

Suddenly I awoke to frenzied shouting. "You are not going to
touch her!"

Brian's voice was at a fever pitch. "You are not going to kill her.
Kill me first!"

I could hear the scuffles in the next room. Brian was shrieking
as he shouted warnings: "Royston is coming to kill you!"

I immediately telephoned the police as Brian fought off the
attack from Royston, who was furious at his foiled murder
attempt. I could hear the rising panic in Brian's voice as he was
beaten with a metal bar. Royston left him bloodied and bruised
before escaping, but he was soon apprehended by police

outside. He was imprisoned overnight and summoned to the Old Bailey again, where I was called to give evidence against him.

For the first time I felt pity and pain for the man who had lost everything. He stood in the dock – his life spent on violence and crime. A man with few principles and few friends who was now openly shamed and rejected. His horrendous reign of terror had finally caught up with him.

There, in the quietened, formal proceedings I forgave him. I forgave him for every terrible deed and despicable act – I forgave him unconditionally as a warm and engulfing peace, that passed every understanding, washed over me. I forgave him as Jesus, my Saviour, forgave me for all my wrongs when he died on the cross. Forgiveness – the total letting go – may not always blunt the pain and distress, but I knew it was the only way. The only way to freedom from this giant of a man who had warred against my soul for nearly 30 years.

Such forgiveness came with the supreme act of God's redeeming grace and mercy. That day I looked Royston full in the face. I looked at the deep crevices of stress and weariness; the heavy furrowed brow and the dark, bewitched eyes. I harboured no bitterness, anger or resentment.

Slowly, I mounted the steps to the witness box. There were questions and cross-questions. I relived the vivid episodes that had twice almost resulted in my death. The interrogations were complete. Royston's sentence would be pronounced.

I pleaded with the judge for leniency. "He said he is going back to Antigua. He is getting on in age. I forgive him and do not want him to return to prison."

He never did go back to a prison cell. Because of my pleas for mercy, the judge gave him an unconditional discharge over a set period, on condition he returned to Antigua. I lived to regret that he was not behind bars.

Instead of returning to Antigua, Royston rented a room at his friend's house in London, but the stalking continued. After months of harassment I saw him lurking outside the police station in Tottenham. A man with a vacant, glazed gaze – aimless and down on his luck.

I faced him defiantly: "I pray that I never, ever see you again – I am leaving you in God's hands." It was the last time I saw him.

Two weeks later there was a knock at the door.

"Mrs Martin, I have got some bad news," said the young police officer.

"Is he dead?" I asked intuitively.

"Yes. He left a note for you."

"I do not want any note," I insisted.

"He is dead." The words echoed again. They breathed relief into my soul. "Is there anyone with you?" the policeman continued.

I called to Gavin: "There is a policeman here."

"I have not done anything, Mum."

"No, I know, but this policeman needs to talk to you."

Gavin stood beside me on the doorstep. There was a chill wind that whipped around us as, together, we were about to hear the fate of a man who had wrought terror and violence against us. There was a momentary silence. The sergeant faced Gavin with a solemn, unflinching gaze. There was no easy way to deliver the news.

"I found your father dead in a car outside North Harringay School this afternoon. I am afraid someone needs to identify him."

Neither of us had the strength for the task. There was no inclination to see and confirm the final passing of Royston.

"Is there anyone else?" asked the policeman.

I finally answered: "There is Sammy – his former boss."

Sammy ran the nightclub in London where Royston worked. I gave the policeman the telephone number.

It was a grisly demise. Royston had parked his car outside the school where he thought I was working that afternoon; he was unaware that I had moved to a new post at Wood Green just days earlier. They could smell the liquor on his breath when they found him slumped over the steering wheel. He had taken a lethal dose of tablets. The car engine was still running – the pipe from the exhaust had filled the vehicle with carbon monoxide fumes. It would have proved fatal within minutes. Identifying the body was gruesome. It was the worst thing Sammy had seen.

Gavin and his friend instinctively returned to Royston's empty flat. There was a vain hope of finding out more, but there was no activity or further clues to Royston's suicide. Instead they found a wad of bank notes – just enough to cover his burial!

Two months before, Sarah had bought me a black dress. It was beautiful but I exclaimed: "Why did you buy me such a dress? You know that my favourite colour is yellow. Why would I even wear this?"

Now the realisation dawned. When the highest court in the land could not curb Royston's insanity, it was as if God himself intervened!

"He cannot hurt you any more, Mum," sighed Sarah.

All the children, apart from Lee, attended the funeral. There was a rift that could not be breached, even at the final passing, for the brutal way his father had treated him. We went to church beforehand to arrange the funeral with the vicar. Royston's threats were still resounding in my ears: "If you take me to any church, I will come back and haunt you."

I decided there would be no service – no time-honoured words from clergy to commend his body to God, no prayers or final commemorations. They were inappropriate to Royston's wishes. Instead I chose an ancient anthem:

Oh God our help in ages past, our hope for years to come,

our shelter from the stormy blast and our eternal home.

The words had a sombre poignancy that we understood. They hung in the hushed atmosphere – true and unchanging for us and countless others across the generations.

Finally, Matthew made a last announcement: "My Dad was not a good husband; he did not treat my Mum properly at all. He was very horrible to her, but he was our Dad. Rest in peace."

Advancing towards the coffin, he hammered a clenched fist once, twice, three times on the wooden lid and departed. In turn Gavin, Marvin and Kevin did the same. We did not attend the cremation in Enfield, north London.

There was no elation or sadness. No tears to mark a mourning. Instead, I thanked God that now, at last, the end had come – although there were the nightmares after his death: they came at least once a week.

Throughout those melancholic years, I had endeavoured to trust a divine and unchanging God. He alone knew my ways, promising to take and make my life through them. No matter the hardship, fear and terrible trauma: I had wanted to live right through them all even though I had, at times, made mistakes when my patience ran out and fear dictated my choices. It was an ongoing prayer – to lean my whole personality, wisdom and understanding on the one who promised to carry me through the deepest treacherous valleys. He was faithful.

Chapter 14 **Never retiring**

Joy runs deeper than despair. *Corrie Ten Boom* [11]

Time waits for no man, and at 58 years old retirement beckoned for me. Despite a short interlude after moving to the UK, I had taught for nearly 40 years. It was the end of the summer term when I rubbed the chalk dust from my hands for the last time and closed the door on Noel Park School in North London. I exited with a school teacher's pension and a hefty lump sum. Much of the latter was gone after repaying an £18,000 debt – the £5,000 I gave to Royston, ensuring a second divorce, and the resulting £13,000 interest!

Retirement did not come easily; I missed the routine, the children and the lessons. During my quest for supply teaching to ease the long and lonely days, there was a telephone call from a colleague informing me of a teaching vacancy. My employment search ended with a permanent part-time job at the school I had left just months earlier – retirement had come and gone!

During the next seven years I also accompanied Class Six on an annual activity holiday to Pendarren. We went by coach to the green Welsh valleys and the commanding peaks of the Brecon Beacons National Park. This veritable jewel in South Wales has a dramatic clarity and beauty of its own. Ancient woodlands and remote wilderness meet with windswept uplands and breathtaking waterfalls. But the true focus for the seven-day break was always the Victorian grey stone outward bound centre, wedged between isolated farmsteads and winding river paths.

The thrilling action-packed agenda – mountaineering, pony trekking, caving, canoeing and abseiling – would include scaling Sugar Loaf Mountain, which stands at nearly 2000 feet, for spectacular views across the Bristol Channel and Black Mountains. Approaching 60 – and beyond in subsequent years, of course – I paddled oars, flexed muscles and gripped the saddle of a sturdy Welsh cob to lead and inspire a class of 20 youngsters.

For the adventurous it was the time of their life, as interpersonal skills developed through tough, shared experiences. For the timid and hesitant there was new confidence when fear, risk and uncertainty were beaten by challenging breakthroughs.

It was usually the boys who missed their mothers and their home comforts. Sobbing at night in the dormitories was eventually silenced when a dab of my perfume on their pillow sent them to sleep. Years of teaching had taught me the art of psychology!

The successive school journeys passed without interruption. I had become a resilient member of the gruelling excursions, even when my last trip was in sight at the age of 65.

One November I was bracing myself for another trip to Pendarren. Matthew was graduating as a teacher, and I learnt that the ceremony coincided with his graduation.

"I did this for you," cried Matthew at the thought of my absence from the event that marked his transition from electrician to teacher. "After all the encouragement you gave me, I did this for you."

Matthew had taken the bold and decisive step of studying at Avery Hill Teacher Training College at New Eltham – following in his older sister's footsteps. He showed unwavering commitment, although it cost him dearly in time, energy and finances, having given up his former career. As an incentive, and with rash generosity, I promised him £1,000 if he graduated as a teacher. Despite having little spare cash, I was able to save a regular monthly sum. The money grew and remained untouched until Matthew needed an unexpected £800 to complete the course.

It was a momentous day when he first crossed the campus – a green oasis in the middle of south-east London. The elegant Victorian mansion had become an elite, international seat of learning for nearly 80 years. Avery Hill had turned out some of the best teachers for future generations, and now Matthew, as well as Sarah, would be added to the list.

I sighed heavily as his voice broke with emotion on the telephone. "Do not get upset. Just wait while I sort this out," I insisted.

The forthcoming ceremony had a double significance, since Sarah would also be presented with her diploma for teaching special education needs, having obtained her postgraduate qualification in teaching some years previously. The event could not be missed.

After I explained the dilemma to the head teacher, she agreed to take my place in Wales, but only until I relieved her immediately after the award ceremony. The fast train from Paddington would take me west in a matter of hours. A waiting chauffeur – who was briefed to look for the only black person on the station – would drive me to the centre to join my pupils.

The graduation soon arrived. I took the connecting underground train to the Barbican Centre, one of the biggest multi-arts centres in Europe. The contemporary concrete and carpeted fortress was separated into halls and arenas with rows upon rows of tiered seating. I finally settled in the appropriate auditorium.

There were tears of joy as Sarah and Matthew, complete with mortar boards and gowns, stepped up to the platform amid the cheers and applause. It was the proudest day of my life. Sarah would later become a department head at a London school, with a teaching career that would span almost 30 years. Matthew would later educate some of the children whose parents I taught years previously, using his advanced teaching skills. The ceremony came as my teaching days in London were almost complete. My relentless battle against injustice and poverty had been worth it. I was privileged to see that it was building a legacy for my children and their children. In subsequent years three of my grandchildren would also study to become teachers.

With the passing of the school year, it was time to sell Montague Road, where I had lived for the past 20 years. I had decided to move back to Thetford – to leave the smog and urban architecture for greener pastures, where there was little reaction to my race or colour. My heart belonged to the Norfolk community that had stretched its strong arms around me and made me feel at home all those years ago. I had been planted and grown in the pleasant streams of life, and I wanted to be transplanted again.

My decision reverberated around the family. I asked Matthew to find me a two-bedroom house without delay, but Sarah was unconvinced. "How can you buy a place when you have not seen it?" she asked.

There could be no arguments. The plan was hatched and soon sealed, with the sale of my London property and the purchase of a home on the north side of Thetford. It was a compact house, joined to another just like it. The rows of neat, regimented boxes, built in the 1970s, lined the wide avenues on the wooded estate. My new home was more than adequate, with a living room, kitchen-cum-dining room and an upstairs bathroom and two bedrooms – one for guests. In the sunny garden, with its solitary, central apple tree, you could hear the distant echo of the Norwich and Cambridge trains.

Initially there was just a bed and a set of garden furniture, since my furniture was temporarily stored in Matthew's garage, and it needed to be reclaimed. It must have looked frugal and inhospitable when my first visitor, the lady next door, joined me for tea the following afternoon. I had written a short invitation to open the door of kindness after a suggestion from the former occupant of my new home.

Reclining on a deck chair in the lounge, Rose relaxed. The years notched against her had taken their toll. Her body was stooped, her legs bent and her hands crooked and gnarled, but she had a resolute gratitude for the years that had moulded her life. As a widow she was isolated and alone, but we soon became companions.

Rose was nearing 90 – she had never spoken to a black person before. He grey eyes widened with astonishment as I unravelled the stories of my former life. She listened and inquired about the hardship and favours, and a faraway land of pineapples and sun-drenched shores. A land she could only dream about while eating my spicy Caribbean chicken and sweet potatoes.

There was a quiet understanding and trust that came with Rose's lack of independence. I took her shopping, ran errands and, when she broke her arm, visited every morning.

"If ever you need help – day or night – just use this to bang on the wall," I told her, placing in her hand a worn, unwanted hockey stick that came from my last school.

Rose, who slept downstairs, took me at my word. Shortly afterwards, I was suddenly awoken in the early hours of the morning. The banging vibrated through the walls and across the bedroom, and I was soon on red alert. Wrapping my heavy coat around me and reaching for my slippers, I grabbed the front door key that Rose had entrusted to me to brave the cold moonlit night.

"Rose, it's all right," I called, turning her key in the lock a moment later. "I am here."

Peering through the shadows of the small front room, I could see the makeshift bed was empty. I turned the light on. Rose was sprawled, motionless, on the floor against the wall, still clutching the hockey stick. I bent down, gently prising the stick from her hands and soothed her ruffled, grey hair. With a strength I did not know I had, I placed my arms around Rose's ample 15-stone frame, lifting her back to bed. After bathing the sore, swollen places on her body, I made her tea and left to the sound of the dawn chorus, visiting regularly until she had recovered from the fall.

Resettling in Thetford was happy and straightforward. The town throbbed with a heart for social reform, enterprise and voluntary initiatives to meet the diverse and challenging cultures it encompassed. It had spearheaded cutting-edge regeneration, demonstrating new prestige, excellence and stability. It had, increasingly, set the seal on its urban and rural geography. Far removed from the former prejudices of my youth in Antigua, it was a place where I believed my children and grandchildren could thrive.

Thetford's residents and environment remained familiar and friendly. Fleeting echoes of the past came as I met countless children I had taught years before. Seasoned by maturity, like fine vintage wines, they now had families and jobs. Roy, Simon and Tony lived nearby. Many of my classroom protégés appeared at my door – older, taller and wiser. Sometimes they came with friends, parents and their own children. They came out of curiosity and to renew acquaintance – recounting events and triumphs while stretching themselves across the sofa or sitting at the kitchen table, animated and thoughtful, with mugs of tea and biscuits.

At 66 years old, with an energy and mind that could not be stilled, I still felt the call to teach. Hearing the fun and laughter from the children's adjacent school playground that autumn was enough to spur me on. Changing my clothes, I walked across the park and through the gate of Drake Primary School. Armed with directions to the head teacher's office, I sat in front of her desk and discussed my teaching prospects while outlining my experience. With a promise to send a Fax to my last school, the head teacher announced that she would be in touch.

Early the next morning, a telephone call resulted in two more years of teaching pupils from nursery to age eight. It was followed with further employment at Raleigh School in Thetford. It was perhaps an unprecedented step; I was still teaching at 70 years old.

The quest to influence positively the lives of thousands of youngsters had exceeded my wildest expectations. It would continue with private tuition and help with the Sunday school and youth club at the town's Church on the Way. Only at 75 did I finally hang up my hat! Yet even now, as I sleep, there are dreams that usher me into the classrooms of the past.

Those dreams were vividly recalled in January 2009 on regional television, when, as a tribute to Barack Obama's achievement as the first black president of the United States, I was interviewed as the first black teacher in Thetford!

"You did us proud, Mum," said Matthew.

Pain and suffering are as nothing when joy drowns every sorrow!

Destiny is no matter of chance. It is not a thing to be waited for; it is a thing to be achieved. [12]

References

[1] **Nin, A**, 1974. Diary of Anais Nin Volume 3 1939-1944: Vol. 3 (1939-1944): Volumes 3 – 1933 (Anais Nin and Gunther Stuhlmann). Available from Waterstone's, WHSmith, Blackwell

[2] **Swindoll, CR**, 1983. Starting Over: Fresh Hope for the Road Ahead, Multnomah.

[3] **Each Campfire Lights Anew**. Song Book – 006 – Scouting Resources. Available from www.scoutingresources.org.uk/downloads/songs_songbook06.pdf

[4] **Walker, T**, 1996. He Knows My Name. Words and music by Tommy Walker@1996 Doulos Publishing. Available from www.tommywalker.net/

[5] **Crosby, FJ** 1890. He Hideth my Soul. Available from www.ccesoline.com/hymns/hehidethmysoul.htm

[6] **Twain, M**, 1884. Adventures of Huckleberry Finn, Chatto & Windus/Charles L. Webster And Company. Republished by Penguin Classics, Black Dog & Leventhal Publishers, Fischer & Salamo, University of California Press, Signet Classics.

[7] **Luther King, M**. Quoted from Don't Try to Live Your Life in One Day! by Johnny Ong. Available from Lulu. com

[8] **Waldo Emerson, R**. The Father of the American Renaissance, by James Poolos, The Rosen Publishing Group.

[9] **C Marshall** 1989. Light in My Darkest Night, Avon Books. Available from www.goodreads.com/book/.../229129.Light_in_My_Darkest_Night

[10] **Moody, DL**. Quoted from Dictionary of Proverbs. Available from books.google.com

[11] **Ten Boom, C**. Quoted from Quote Unquote (A Hardbook of Quotations) by M P Singh, Lotus Press.

[12] **Bryan, WJ**. Quoted from The Big Game: 10 Strategies for Winning at Life, Scott MacMillan, Llewellyn Publications

Lord, I'm coming home

Are you running from God today? Stop, turn around, come back home. He is waiting to welcome you. He says: "Turn back to me" (Revelation 3:30). Come; there's no sin He can't forgive and no addiction that Jesus' love can't help you overcome.

James MacDonald writes: "Maybe you've done something you think is beyond (God's) mercy... or someone hurt you and you don't understand why God let it happen... maybe you'd rather live by your own rules. I don't know why you're running, but I know one thing: you're tired. You're so used to this flight pattern you can't imagine life any differently. Jesus talked about a son taking off from his dad's house. After this runner's rise and fall, he woke up one day in a pig-sty wondering, "How'd I get here? I need to go back but what'll my dad say? Have you ever thought, *"if I come back how will God receive me?" Some people think He wouldn't care one way or the other... But that's not how Jesus described His Father... those feet pounding the pavement are God's feet running towards you. He's been scanning the horizon for a glimpse of you... and now that He sees you He's in a full run.* "While he was still a long way off, his father... ran and embraced him. God put this in (the Bible –Luke 15:20) so every runner will know what to expect when they reverse course."

"God... devises ways to bring us back when we have been separated from him." (2 Sam 14:14). Can you feel a divine tug at your heart? Isn't it time you stopped running, turned around and said: "Lord, I'm coming home."

Based on an excerpt from: *The Word for Today*, free issues being available in the UK and Republic of Ireland from United Christian Broadcasters, Operations Centre, Westport Road, Stoke-on-Trent, ST6 4JF. ucb@ucb.co.uk or visit www.ucb.co.uk